THE BUNDY SECRETS

Hidden Files Of America's
Worst Serial Killer

By
Kevin M. Sullivan

THE BUNDY SECRETS published by:
WILDBLUE PRESS

P.O. Box 102440
Denver, Colorado 80250

Publisher Disclaimer: Any opinions, statements of fact or fiction, descriptions, dialogue, and citations found in this book were provided by the author, and are solely those of the author. The publisher makes no claim as to their veracity or accuracy, and assumes no liability for the content.

WILDBLUE PRESS is registered at the U.S. Patent and Trademark Offices.

978-1-942266-85-3   Trade Paperback ISBN
978-1-942266-86-0   eBook ISBN

Cover Design and Interior Formatting by Elijah Toten Totencreative.com

Other WildBlue Press Books By Kevin Sullivan

VAMPIRE: *The Richard Chase Murders*
http://wbp.bz/vampirea

KENTUCKY BLOODBATH: *Ten Bizarre Tales
of Murder From The Bluegrass State*
http://wbp.bz/kba

THE TRAIL OF TED BUNDY:
Digging Up The Untold Stories
http://wbp.bz/trailbundya

This book is dedicated to all those who labor in the researching and writing of books, so that you, the future reader, may have the same knowledge they've acquired, long after they're gone.

INTRODUCTION

This is the third and final book in a trilogy of books about the life of Ted Bundy. My first book on the case, *The Bundy Murders: A Comprehensive History*, was an in-depth biography of Ted Bundy. My second book, *The Trail of Ted Bundy: Digging up the Untold Stories*, provided, like my first book, new, important, and never before published information on the case, as well as an updated look at how these locations appear today.

With this final work, however, I'm doing something that I never dreamed I'd have a chance to do: reproduce various entire portions of the official record so that others can read and appreciate all that's really in there. In reality, most people will never lay eyes on the record, despite it being available to the public. It's not that they can't peruse them, as there are archives that house these materials and they're open to the public (except for Utah's records, where you actually have to know someone to lay your hands on the really important files!). However, that's not what people do. They wait for people like me to pull it out of the archives, do the interviewing of individuals, and put it all neatly together and get it down on the printed page so they can purchase the book. I know it's this way, as this is what I do every time I purchase a book. We let other folks gather the knowledge and then we wait for the book. This is just the way it is.

Within the pages of this book, you'll read complete reports, entire letters, and various communications in the same way it came before the eyes of the investigators. It is a fascinating look into the Bundy case from a unique perspective. Along with the record, I will have commentary throughout, aiding your understanding of the text, and adding clarification where needed.

I also have new and important testimony from a number of people who were kind enough to share their stories with me so that I can share them with you. Most of these testimonies have never before been put to print, and, as always, it enhances what we know about Ted Bundy and the case in general, especially the long-hidden story of Louise Cannon, who had a conversation with Bundy only two hours before he would kidnap and murder Melissa Smith, only four blocks from where they were standing.

Despite the passage of over 40 years, not everyone is able to open up and speak about those days, and I understand it. As such, I am extremely grateful for those who do open that door and allow me to peer within, and for that, I (and you) are eternally grateful.

Kevin M. Sullivan
Louisville, KY

PREFACE

If I could say only one thing about the official record of the Ted Bundy case, it would be this: It is rich in information. It is an inexhaustible source, almost bottomless in its density of material. What follows is the record of the Ted Bundy case files, from the various states where Bundy committed abduction and murder, or was suspected of doing so. Without question, the case files, housed in the archives in various states, are a gold mine of information and insight concerning Ted Bundy and his crimes. Indeed, no matter how much material I used for my first book on the case, there is information here that neither I, nor any other author of any of the Bundy books has used. It's just impossible to make use of it all, as the book would have to be in the tens of thousands of pages!

Not only did I pull extensively from these case files when first writing *The Bundy Murders*, and then, to a lesser extent, my second book on the case, *The Trail of Ted Bundy*, but I have returned to them for this last book for a very special reason. During my original research period (2006 through late 2008) for *The Bundy Murders*, each time I received the case files from the respective states, I was transported back to the world of the investigators who were so diligently hunting a killer of women and girls that turned out to be Theodore Robert Bundy. Being rich in information (and we're talking many thousands of pages), I perused the material, picking and choosing the facts pertaining to Bundy and his victims that I needed for the book. Notice I said picking and choosing. The more I delved into the files, the more I remember thinking, "I wish the reader could have the opportunity to see these actual reports that contain so much interesting material about this killer and his victims." That, of course, was just wishful thinking, as I understood that only seasoned researchers would see what I was now seeing. While I put many things into my first book on Bundy (it is crammed with facts), there just isn't any way to include it all. Indeed, my personal case file material of the Bundy case is so extremely large, that I actually, for this third book, found information in the record that I'd missed the first and even second time I researched the case!

Without question, the original case files of the Bundy murders are so extensive that even with the publication of this book you'll still only be seeing a small portion of what's out there. However, what is here has been carefully selected by me – your guide- so that you will be able to experience some of what I experienced when this massive journey began back in 2006. It is an eye-opening experience, and one that will enrich those who have been seeking additional information on this case. You'll be viewing what was at one time extremely classified info, carefully guarded by the police as they did the tough work of hunting an elusive killer of women.

A note: there is very little duplicating of information I've already used in my first two books on Ted Bundy. However, in certain circumstances, I will be repeating informative quotes (extremely briefly) from those portions of the case file so that readers who haven't read my first two works will be getting enough of the story to understand what is going on in the passage; doing this will keep them from feeling that something is missing. Those who have closely followed what has now become a trilogy, however, will find this last book to be filled with almost exclusively new information; as well as never-before published accounts from those who knew Bundy, or were friends of or worked with the victims, as well as those who were part of the investigation. Throughout the record, I will be adding necessary commentary that will expand on the issue at hand, and this will give you greater insight into the case. In addition, to avoid any confusion during the record portion of the book, my words will appear in italics so that it will be easily recognizable to the reader as to what are my words, and what belongs to the record.

The following reports are from the official record, and with few exceptions, I'll be adding full reports that are of interest. In some instances, only partial reports will be included, but in these instances, that which has been left out stems from either it being published in my previous books, or because of a single sheet which might be missing (a rare occurrence). There will be times when you'll notice an ellipsis that is not a part of the record, but placed there by me, and this pertains to an illegible word or words (handwritten notes from the investigators, etc.), and this is the best way to denote such unfortunate losses of content. Many of these reports were created after Bundy became a suspect. Where an ellipsis is part of the record, I will note it. There are no corrections in grammar, spelling, or punctuation in any of the material I'll be using from the reports, except where an obvious word has been left out that, without it, may obscure the true meaning to the reader.

It is also important to note that the actual name of Bundy's Seattle girlfriend was Liz Kloepfer, and that Kloepfer's name (known as Liz Kendall from her book, *The Phantom Prince*, and referred to in my previous books as Kendall) is redacted, as is her exact Seattle address (some reports mistakenly leave her address in the report, and I point this out where it occurs). When you see this, you can fill in the blanks. Whenever I have comments within the record section, I will preface it with "Author's note," and as mentioned above, my words will be in italics, giving the reader an unmistakable line of demarcation as to what are my comments and what is the official record.

Also, whether you're a seasoned Bundy murders scholar or someone new to the story, I am providing a list of his known victims (known, because he admitted to the murders, or because there is overwhelming evidence connecting him to them). Be aware, however, that most investigators who worked the Bundy case (and most of the Bundy writers, including myself) believe Ted Bundy killed more women and young girls than he admitted to at the end of his life. Indeed, he admitted to killing eleven in Washington but would only give the names of eight. In Utah, he confessed to murdering eight but provided the names of only five. Of course, I believe that there were more victims that he wouldn't talk about.

And finally, a note concerning the layout of information contained within this book. Unlike a biography that must follow events in a chronological order (for without it there would be chaos), the numerous case files contained within this book are presented in several ways and you will occasionally notice the information may jump around a bit. For example, if a murder occurs in 1974, but a particular witness isn't interviewed until 1975, these reports may be contained in different sections of the book. Or, if it's advantageous to include nearly all of a detective's reports sequentially (as in the case of Jerry Thompson), there will still be Jerry Thompson reports found in other sections of this book due to the overlapping he had with other detectives on the case. Lastly, I have attempted to occasionally "bunch up" certain pages and brief reports with each other as they are not only interesting, but in these cases (due to the type of material being presented), it will "read' better, in my opinion. So, if you're very familiar with the Bundy case and the cast of characters, you shouldn't miss a beat, as it were, as the reports come in groupings and then have a tendency to go off in another direction before coming back again. If you're newer to the case, just buckle up and after a while it will all start to jell.

What follows are the victims that we can say with certainty were murdered by Theodore Robert Bundy, including the dates and locations where they went missing:

- Lynda Ann Healy: (21) February 1, 1974, Seattle, Washington. Lynda was choked into unconsciousness by Ted Bundy in the middle of the night in a house she shared with other University of Washington coeds.

- Donna Gail Manson: (19) March 12, 1974, disappeared from the campus of Evergreen State College as she walked to the library to attend a jazz concert and dance. Bundy would later admit to her abduction and murder.

- Susan Elaine Rancourt: (18) April 17, 1974, disappeared at night while walking back to her dorm room on the campus of Central Washington State College in Ellensburg, Washington.

- Roberta Kathleen Parks: (22) May 6, 1974, disappeared after entering the cafeteria at Oregon State University around 11:00 p.m. Bundy convinced her to leave with him under some pretense or ruse.

- Brenda Carol Ball: (22) June 1, 1974. Brenda was last seen at the Flame Tavern in Burien, south of Seattle, and Bundy would later connect himself to her murder.

- Georgann Hawkins: (18) June 11, 1974. Georgann encountered Bundy walking on crutches in a Seattle alley behind a row of frat and sorority houses, and convinced her to help him carry some items to his car one block away.

- Janice Ann Ott: (23) July 14, 1974. Janice encountered Bundy at Lake Sammamish State Park and disappeared after agreeing to leave with him and assist him with his sailboat.

- Denise Marie Naslund: (19) July 14, 1974. Denise encountered Bundy a at Lake Sammamish bathroom around 4:00 p.m. and left with him after he presented her with an unknown ruse. She was Bundy's second and last victim of the day.

- Nancy Wilcox: (16) October 2, 1974. Bundy attacked her while she was walking down a street at night in Holiday, Utah. She was raped and strangled, and her body was never recovered.

- Melissa Smith: (18) October 18, 1974. Melissa disappeared after leaving a pizza restaurant around 10:00 p.m. in Midvale, Utah. Bundy was also there and followed her out, according to one witness. Her body was recovered weeks later.

- Laura Ann Aime: (17) disappeared around midnight along a dark portion of Highway 89 near Lehi, Utah. Apparently, Bundy picked her up while she was hitchhiking. Her body was recovered in American Fork Canyon.

- Debra Kent: (17) November 8, 1974. After Bundy lost Carol DaRonch, his intended victim, he drove to Viewmont High School in Bountiful, Utah where a play was in progress. Here, he would abduct Debra Kent as she left the play early to pick up her brother. Bundy admitted his role in her murder.

- <u>Caryn Eileen Campbell:</u> (26) January 12, 1975. Caryn Campbell disappeared from the outdoor second floor hallway of the Wildwood Inn. By ruse, Ted Bundy encountered her as she stepped off the elevator and convinced her to leave with him. Her body was found off Owl Creek Road some two miles away from the Wildwood Inn. Bundy gave details about this murder.

- <u>Julie Cunningham:</u> (26) March 15, 1975. Julie Cunningham was walking to a tavern in Vail, Colorado when she encountered Ted Bundy who was feigning an injury. Agreeing to help him to his car with his things, he knocked her out cold with a crowbar as she leaned into his VW to place the items on the seat. Authorities know roughly where her remains are located, but they never recovered the body. I was also told that her parents would like her to remain where she is, and thus far that has been the case. However, I was also informed that building in the area may one day disturb her grave.

- <u>Denise Oliverson:</u> (25) April 6, 1975. Denise Oliverson disappeared from Grand Junction, Colorado while riding her bicycle in the city. Bundy told investigators that he killed her and dumped her body in the Colorado River five miles west of Grand Junction as he made his way back to Utah. Her body was never recovered.

- <u>Lynette Culver:</u> (12) May 6, 1975. Ted Bundy came upon Lynette as she was leaving Alameda Junior High for lunch, and after a brief chat, she agreed to go with him. They drove back to the Holiday Inn where the killer still had a room, and he murdered her by drowning her in the bathtub. Bundy admitted placing her body in a river about five miles north of Pocatello. Her remains have never been found.

- <u>Susan Curtis:</u> (15) June 28, 1975. Susan Curtis was attending a youth conference being held at Brigham Young University in Provo, Utah. She was last seen walking the outdoor pathway to her room. Accurate details as to her abduction and murder are unknown, however, only minutes before Bundy was put to death, he admitted he had murdered the young girl.

- <u>Margaret Bowman</u>: (21) January 15, 1978. Beaten about the head with a log as she slept in her bed in the Chi Omega sorority house in Tallassee, Florida. Bundy then murdered her through strangulation.

- <u>Lisa Levy</u>: (20) January 15, 1978. Like Margaret Bowman, Lisa Levy was bludgeoned about the head with the log (this is the same log that Bundy carried from Chi Omega to Dunwoody), sexually assaulted, and strangled to death.

- <u>Kimberly Diane Leach: (12)</u> February 9, 1978. Young Kim Leach was abducted by Ted Bundy from Lake City Junior High School as she was walking alone from a portable building to the main building. Bundy, who'd been trolling the school for a little while, spotted the young girl and made his move. Her decomposed body was found almost two months later some 45 miles out of Lake City, Florida.

THE RECORD

The Washington, Utah and Colorado Reports

Author's note: It's important for the reader to keep in mind that when the murders began in Washington State in early 1974, it would take over a year and a half before Ted Bundy became the primary suspect in the investigation. Once that happened, it wouldn't be long before the authorities in all the locations where Bundy had killed would each have their epiphany and their eyes would forever open as to who was actually the killer of all these missing women. It was Ted Bundy, and everyone knew it. However, in the months preceding these revelations, the overwhelming frustration of the Washington cops sometimes rose to the surface. This wasn't abnormal, of course, as these frustrations were commonly expressed privately among the investigators as the case dragged on without there being any real clues that could lead them to this strange and crafty destroyer of women. When such frustrations were voiced publicly, those in the community took notice. For many, it just heightened their fears as they understood that the killer might escape detection altogether.

What follows is from an article published in the Tacoma News Tribune on Sunday, July 28, 1974, and quotes seasoned investigator, Herb Swindler, of the Seattle Police Department and captain of the missing person's unit. Although I will not be quoting the entire article, I will highlight enough of it to convey just how much they were at rope's end by the end of July of 1974. Keep in mind that by this time, they had no answers for the vanishings of Lynda Ann Healy, Georgann Hawkins, Brenda Ball, Donna Gail Manson, Denise Naslund, and Janice Ott.

"I lie awake at night thinking about those girls…I have a daughter too…I can sit here and spin theories all day," Swindler is quoted as saying, "but none of them work without facts to go on…I wouldn't like to tell you some of the horrible suspicions I have – some of the strange theories I've wondered about…I'm at the point now where I'll do anything, no matter how improbable; we're as frustrated now as when we began."

Dante's Tavern, a place both Ted Bundy and Lynda Ann Healy frequented in the University District in Seattle. This picture was taken in July 2015, and one month later the inside of the tavern was destroyed by a fire.

Author's note: The following information concerns the abduction of Lynda Ann Healy, snatched from her bed in the middle of the night from the rooming house she shared with other coeds in the University District in Seattle. It is, in my opinion, by far the strangest abduction I've ever encountered in my years of reading or writing true crime. Indeed, Bundy set records as a serial killer throughout his career as a murderer. The truest thing we can say, as we look back on him, is that, as a killer, he was completely unpredictable. The methods by which he would abduct his victims, as well as his almost total lack of fear of the authorities or society (he didn't mind being seen!), made him an exceedingly dangerous predator. Given these peculiarities, it's surprising that it took as long as it did to apprehend him.

On the evening prior to her early morning abduction, Lynda and several friends walked the few blocks from their rooming house at 5517 Twelfth St. N.E., to Dante's Tavern, located at 5300 Roosevelt Way N.E. Bundy was most likely in the tavern, had spotted the party, and followed them back home, keeping a safe distance so as not to be discovered. He waited a number of hours before entering the house and attacking her.

In July of 2015, when I visited the home where Lynda Ann Healy had lived with her housemates, it appeared much the same as it did in 1974. The same was true for Dante's Tavern, a tavern that was still owned by the same family for over 50 years. As I toured the place and photographed the inside, including the infamous "Bundy sofa," I remember thinking it was very interesting and surprising that Dante's was still in business after all these years. Then, just a month later in August, an electrical fire destroyed much of the inside of the bar. As of this writing, August 2016, the latest notice is "permanently closed".

Seattle Police Bulletin

City of Seattle Washington

FEBRUARY 11, 1974

MISSING PERSON

HEALY, LYNDA ANN USWF 21

DOB: 7/3/52, 5'7", 115 lbs., slim build,

Long brown hair, blue eyes.

Nativity, Portland, Oregon

1/2" scar on bridge of nose.

Wearing turquoise rings on each ring finger.

Subject was last seen at 2400 hours, 1/31/74, when she left main floor of her home to proceed to her basement bedroom.

Subject wearing blue jeans, white, smock-type blouse with blue trim, brown vinyl waffle stompers, brown belt. Missing from her room is a red backpack containing possibly a yellow ski cap and yellow gloves, miscellaneous books. ID was found intact in the subject's bedroom. Subject is talkative but afraid to be alone.

Any and all information should be sent to Detectives Ted Fonis and Wayne Dorman, Homicide Unit, Seattle Police Department, re: Case # 74-5953.

Author's note: What follows are three brief reports pertaining to the double abduction from Lake Sammamish on July 14, 1974, which took the lives of Janice Ott and Denise Naslund. The first two reports contain information given by the two hunters who stumbled upon Bundy's Issaquah dumpsite. The third report details a rather bizarre event that turned out to be a prank.

Statement of Sgt. Edward O. Mott #132, Issaquah Police Dept. Issaquah, Washington.

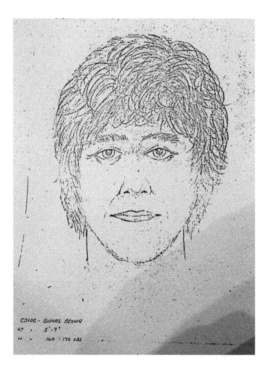

The composite drawing of the suspect who led two women away from Lake Sammamish State Park in July 1974

At 0958 my dept. radio advised me to contact a citizen at the P.D. ref. to possibly to finding the remains of a body, in/or near the city of Issaquah. R/O contacted a Mr. Hammons, Elzie Alvin, DOB 11/7/16, 25th St. N.E. Seattle, Wash. He stated that he had just run across what he believed to be a human skull and remains. I advised him to lead the way in his vehicle and I would follow. Mr. Hammons directed R/O east of the city limits and on an old service road north of I-90. Officer Peach met with me to check out the report. On the service road north of I-90 I contacted three other subjects. They were Rankin, Elza Everett DOB 1-6-04, Hartsfield, Jeffery Lewis...11317 238th S.W. Edmonds, WA. And Darling, Roger Delbert...USS Morton...San Fran. Calif. I had Mr. Hartsfield guide me to the scene. I had Officer Peach lead the way then Hartsfield then myself we were guided to the north of this service road and up a short bluff. There I observed what appeared to be a human skull and remains. The three of us then walked down to the service road and I had all persons back their vehicles... *(Author's note: This is unclear, and obviously, information is missing from this report)*

Author's note: What follows is the transcript of the statement given by Elza E. Rankin:

I, Elza Everett Rankin 1-6-1904 of 11717 25th Ave. N.E. Seattle...give this statement to Off. C.M. Wilson Issaquah P.D.

My friend & I (Elsie Hammond) arrived in this area to do some grouse hunting at about 7:00 a.m. 8-2-74. We drove around the woods for about 2 – 2 ½ hours. At about 9:30 Elsie stated he wanted to do some more hunting. I waited at the car for him to return. He returned approx 15 minutes later. Elsie stated he had found a human skull. We both went with another lad back to where he had seen the skull. I first saw the hair about twenty feet from where the skull was. I then saw some type of rib section ½ way from hair to skull. Then went to look at the skull. We then went back to our car & Elsie went to report what we found.

Author's note: The following report concerns an odd prank performed in exceedingly bad taste given the circumstances. Its strange aspect and connection to this case make its inclusion worthwhile.

City of Issaquah

Issaquah, Washington

Police Department

On approximately October 19, 1974, at approximately 0200 hours, this officer was advised by a citizen of a possible body in the roadway on I-90 at the train trestle. This officer went up with the citizen and observed a dummy in the eastbound lane of I-90. This was approximately the third dummy this officer has seen below the trestle. I took the dummy and threw it in the woods by the trestle. Two days later this officer went back and looked at the dummy close-up and saw that it had a white sweatshirt with a caricature of two pigs "humping", one was labeled Smith and the other Mott. This was on the front of the shirt. Also on the front in black felt pen was the wording "Ted Lives". On the sleeve it appeared to read "Ted + IPD + Smith + Mott". This was difficult to read though. The sweatshirt was white and appeared to be small or medium size. I took the sweatshirt back to the station as I thought Mott or Smith might be interested in the caricature of the pig. I showed this to Sergeant Mott and Paula Ralph. I then disposed of the sweatshirt. There was also a pair of pants I left at the trestle. They were tan-brown corduroy of medium size and good condition... The handwriting appeared to be juvenal (sic). This officer checked on the pants on November 8, 1974. They had been removed from underneath the trestle.

Officer: Keith L. Moon

Author's note: The following letter is from Tim Clancy to Larry Voshall (Voshall knew Bundy but didn't particularly like him. Clancy, on the other hand, was a friend of Ted's and they worked a number of political campaigns together in Washington State). For The Bundy Murders I used only a very small portion of this correspondence, but for this book, I will be using the entire letter. Also, a correction to my first Bundy book: I incorrectly stated that Tim Clancy was living in Italy when he received the communication, when, in fact, he was on vacation there, and within two weeks would be in Paris, France. The envelope is dated November 13, 1975.

Dear Larry, Wow! That's unbelievable. Considering the type of mentality of the person or persons involved in these bizarre murders, it's frightening; but to actually believe that such a person is an acquaintance, I dare say a confident (sic), of ours is more than I can comprehend. And yet... *(Author's note: This ellipsis is original to the letter and not added by me to denote missing information.)*

I will try to relay to you my initial reaction and thoughts. As such, I don't believe my correspondence at this time should go beyond you, in that I only received your letter this p.m. I do believe further thought should be given on my part as to more particulars before notifying the authorities. Initial reactions & opinions have a habit of becoming fact with some.

I first met Ted Bundy in June of '68 on the Draft Rockefeller Campaign in Seattle. He was working on the A. Fletcher campaign during the day and at Safeway as a night stock boy. I was the State Youth Chairman, and I made him my Seattle area chairman. He was living in the U-District in one of those back street apts. Ted and I spent a lot of time together that summer, and as far as I know, I was the only young politico he got along with very well. He did not like the original AFW crowd much. I recall that he speaks fluent Mandarin Chinese having taken a national defense funded crash course at Stanford at some...time. I also recall that occasionally he would mimic an English accent in jest. I recall an incident in the '68 campaign in which Ted stood up in an open meeting and challenged...KIRO's refusal to run Fletcher's TV ads and ...relationship to their Mormon ownership. He does not lack balls. After the campaign, he drifted out of circulation, but I ran into...in 1969, I believe. He was living with a group of guys and he mentioned that though he didn't indulge, these jokers were shooting up heroin. You could never trust what Ted would say, and I doubt that it was true. He always seemed to be saying things for affect. Though I may have run into him sometime later, the next period which sticks out was in Spokane, spring of 1973. I understand the political sensitivity of this since at the time he was Ross D's A.A. nothing particular stands out at that time. I was finishing up at law school & we merely had lunch. He was just as cynical as always. Ted is one of the great cynics of our time. I could never understand how he could work on the projects he did if he felt the way he said.

After that my mind is a total blank on Mr. Bundy. I believe when I was working on the Kramer Congressional race in early summer of 1974, Ted came by and we had a few drinks, but nothing is too vivid or extraordinary. All I knew is that he was going to school in Utah (law?) and visiting his folks in Tacoma (?).

As you can see my latest knowledge is skimpy and frankly I know virtually nothing of his whereabouts in 1974-1975. In the far recesses of my mind I know I have seen him more than I now recall. I will continue to search.

As for a few personal remarks, which are mere observations and gut reactions. I guess Ted B. could be "Ted" but I don't want to believe so, none of us do. Bundy is a strange bird, and if anyone fits the description of enigmatic, he does. Maybe that's why we (from your letter I gather you think so) believe he could be the sick fiend. I personally never saw him in the company of a young woman, though I do recall him attempting to pick up some friends of mine. He is handsome, has flair and is a sharp dresser, but he comes on too strong.

I apologize for having no more information, but in recent years I haven't known him well. I'm certain you and the authorities have contacted everyone you can think of, but just in case, John Fratt knew him in the early days. He may be helpful in doing a further psych of Ted's personality. Ask him about his old girlfriend Jan…and her roommate Jean. I believe Ted took or tried to take Jean out. Good luck! I have mentioned that I have done this in one day and am certain I cannot recall everything. I will contact you again. As for further developments please write American Express, 11 Rue Scribe, Paris, France. We should be there in about two weeks. Let me know then if you think I should cut this thing short and come home to help out somehow.

Needless to say this has not really hit me yet, but I hope we can all keep an objective and unbiased viewpoint on it. I am certain a lot has passed since you wrote your letter & possibly the situation is resolved.

Regardless, good luck and keep in touch.

Tim Clancy (no E)

Author's note: The following reports were written by King County Police Det. Kathleen McChesney on August 26, 1975, and September 8, 1975. Although the name of the interviewee is redacted from the reports, we know it is Bundy's girlfriend, Liz Kloepfer (also known by her pseudonym of Liz Kendall). They are filled with a lot of interesting information which makes sense now because of what we know about Bundy, but did not have the same impact prior to Bundy's unmasking.

8-26-75 1015 hrs. R/O had personal contact with (redacted) in this office. She had quite a bit of information regarding TED BUNDY. She stated that they met in September of 1969 at the Sandpiper Tavern in the U District which is now the Rainbow Tavern….(redacted) stated that she and TED broke up one time in 1972 when he was dating a girl he worked with at the Mental Health Center at Harborview. They were broken up for a couple of weeks…Several years ago she found a brown bag full of women's clothing. At another time she found under the seat of his Volkswagen a hatchet. On a third occasion she found a knife that she was advised was given to him by a friend. This knife was in the glove compartment of (redacted)'s car. (Redacted) also observed a meat tenderizer and a meat cleaver as Ted was packing to go to law school in Utah last fall. According to (redacted) TED had been to Utah three times – in December of 1969 and the summers of 1970 and 1971 or 1972…The knife that TED had he stated he had received from MARLIN VORTMAN who lived in the Magnolia area.

(Redacted) indicated that TED had credit cards with Standard Oil and Nordstrom Best; that his checking account was with Rainier Bank in the University District. She advised that he had a friend named TERRY in Ellensburg whom they visited in the summertime. She said that on one occasion he borrowed her car to go to Richland, which she believes was in the summer of 1970. (Redacted) also found a stolen television set in his room, confronted him with the fact, and he admitted to her that he had stolen it and would not do this again...During the past month TED'S brother RICHARD visited him in Salt Lake. TED crated a bicycle and packed it back with RICHARD on the airplane. When (redacted) questioned TED about this he asked her "what bike?" and (redacted) has not seen the bicycle.

Author's note: Liz, without Bundy's knowledge or permission, retrieved cancelled checks for the time period of April of 1974 from his apartment and brought them in to Det. McChesney to look over. Bundy had made purchases from Campus Creamery and Ness Flowers in the U District, as well as from Ernst Hardware and QFC Food Stores in University Village. Bundy also wrote a check to Freeway Volkswagen.

9-8-75 In 1972 in the summer he worked at Harborview Hospital in the Mental Health Unit. He dated a girl named SANDY GWINN at that time. Upon completing that he worked for Governor Evans' campaign in Seattle. In the fall of 72 he began working for the Seattle Crime Commission and in March of 73 began working for the Republican Party in Olympia, to which he commuted. In Sept. of 73 he began law school at the University of Puget Sound as a night student; he attended Winter and Spring Quarters. His possible schedule was Monday, Wednesday and Friday for the first semester, leaving Seattle at 5:00 and returning at 11:00 p.m. He didn't go down to the law school just for study, there was a study group here in Seattle and they would go to various houses to study. He would also go to the University Law Library. In the summer of 1974 TED worked for the Dept. of Emergency Services in Olympia, beginning approximately June 11th.

He worked on the budget and worked on Monday through Friday. Sometimes he would stay at his parents' house, his house, or FREIDA'S house – he was usually in Seattle on the weekends. This job lasted until Sept. of 1974. Redacted does not does not remember what TED did between the end of law school and the Dept. of Emergency Services job but she believes he did not have a job at that time. He started applying to law schools in his senior year of 1972 and applied to ten. He received one acceptance from the University of Utah but did not want to attend there. He also applied to Berkeley, San Francisco, University of Washington, and possibly University of Oregon, and Willamette University. He re-applied a second time to some of the above. In March of 1974 he called Utah and they said they would accept his application as a new student (this means he would return to Utah as a freshman, not having advised them he had been a law student the previous year.) TED said that he did not like the commuting atmosphere of the University of Puget Sound Law School. TED did not belong to any other outside organizations other than the Republican Party and CHECC. He did not belong to any particular athletic teams although he did visit the intramural building quite often. He was very much interested in handball, and would play with whomever might be at the athletic center. He has an aunt in Philadelphia – her name is AUDY, and an uncle in Arkansas. He visited in Utah at Christmas of 1969 where he apparently drove with her friends and she met him down there. Part of this indicated that he flew to Utah, I believe this information is correct that he drove with some friends of (redacted). During the summer of 70, (redacted) and TED drove together to Utah – they would go to Eastern Washington, through Yakima, south through Baker, Oregon, they would not connect through Vancouver or Portland in driving to Utah. Between March and Sept. of 73 Bundy flew to San Francisco on business for the Republican Party. When not at law school he would usually visit/study with (redacted) go to the IMA Bldg. with JOHN NEELER who also lived at FREIDA ROGERS' house in the U District. He did not have a locker at the Intramural Athletic Bldg. He has no brothers or sisters who attend college and no friends at any out of state colleges. His cousin, JOHN, attended the University of Mississippi and also a school in Arkansas... In the fall of 1973 (redacted) observed a sack of clothing in TED's room one night while he was at law school. The only piece of clothing she actually observed was a white bra which was a very large size. (redacted) assumed these to be FREIDA's clothes and did not look at them any further. FREIDA cleaned TED's room every Friday and TED's door was generally unlocked. During 1972 (redacted) observed a television and stereo in TED's room – TED admitted to her later that he had stolen these things but he would not do something like that again. (Redacted) also observed an electric typewriter in TED's room which she stated he had bought from the Republican Headquarters. TED is described by (redacted) as materialistic – he enjoyed listening to music and still has the stereo and TV. In May or June of 1974, (redacted) observed crutches in TED's room – TED stated they belonged to ERNST ROGERS, his landlord who had a problem with his feet. TED was going to return them for ERNST or ERNST gave them to him, (redacted) could not remember. (Redacted) also observed an Ace bandage that TED had obtained when TED broke his foot while going to Temple Univ. She also observed plaster of Paris in his room on an occasion. Ted had a friend named TERRY STORWICK from Ellensburg who attended Central in '72. On one occasion TED drove to Richland and drove (redacted)'s car and stopped and stayed with TERRY. TERRY attended Wilson High School and lived in Tacoma. He has since graduated but was living in student housing with his wife in Ellensburg while attending Central. (Redacted) knew of no contacts TED had at Oregon State Univ. although she believes they went through Corvallis on one occasion when they were returning from Utah and looked around the campus. TED has never done any caretaking for any party. On New Year's of 1974 TED attended a New Year's party at Crystal Mountain at the cabin of a law school friend. He stayed overnight at that time. TED's family has a cabin at Crescent Lake and during '74 the cabin was constructed; prior to that there was a lean-to and tent structure that remained up all year round. (Redacted) visited Crescent Lake approximately three times in the summer of 74. TED's parents go to the cabin often. (Redacted) stated that TED went to Crescent Lake went one time overnight to get away from things. To get to the cabin you go through Gig Harbor, the cabin is west of Gig Harbor about 10 – 15 minutes on the lake by some other houses. It takes approximately one and a half hours from Seattle. TED owns a 35 mm camera but does not develop his own film. She saw a film canister with black tape around it on one occasion in his room but did not open it…(redacted) stated she had never observed any pornography in TED's room; that birthdays with his family were not particularly special occasions…He went to a Laundromat on University Way N.E.…Often when out driving, TED would look for roads away from the main roads. He didn't study much on the weekends, did study at the law library at the University of Washington once or twice; and once or twice studied at the University of Puget Sound Law Library. He did go camping on one occasion by Mt. Rainier – he doesn't hunt, fish, hike or backpack according to (redacted). He used to ski a lot more and never went away for a skiing weekend.

1500 hrs. R/O received phone call from SANDY GWINN…

She is employed as manager of the Stanford Court Hotel in San Francisco. SANDY stated that she met TED BUNDY in the summer of 1972 when she worked with him at Harborview Mental Health. She worked with him for several months and went out with him for about four or five months. She stated that his girlfriend kept threatening suicide and this presented a problem and they broke up. She stated she saw (redacted) or that (redacted) had come to TED's house when she was in TED's room and this presented quite a problem. She stated they went to Pier 70 and a couple of other restaurants and also a black nightclub. She felt that TED was very concerned about mental problems. She remembers going on a picnic with him at a river south of Seattle near Olympia – it was a secluded area – they had intended to go to Ocean Shores, however, it was foggy and they had a picnic instead at this other location. They went in SANDY's car as TED did not have a car at the time. She describes TED as being a friendly type. She remembers bike riding at Green Lake with him several times – she remembers one occasion when they drove to Lake Sammamish to look for someone who TED knew but TED wasn't able to find the house; she believes it was someone in the family, like the grandmother. She stated that he had some strange attitudes and remembered that he did not have any men friends...He told SANDY he felt inferior to her and did not want to come to SANDY's home for that reason. He always wore dark colored clothes, navy and brown. They went sailing on Lake Washington several times after renting a sailboat at Portage Bay. TED loved to sail very much. In the summer after graduation he worked at Harborview for about six months. SANDY stopped working at Harborview in Sept. of 72 and stopped seeing TED primarily due to (redacted)'s suicide threats. TED told her he had broken up with (redacted) prior to his seeing SANDY. TED was always broke. On one occasion SANDY went with TED to see Mango Santa Maria near Jackson Street. He enjoyed her dependence on him and enjoyed seeing her hassled by blacks. On one occasion she dropped him off at the corner near (redacted)'s house because he saw (redacted) go by while he was in SANDY's car. He tried out techniques on patients during counseling, but seemed to be without compassion. He was very physically oriented and enjoyed touching SANDY. He had a warm smile but they did not get involved physically...she describes him as sexually aggressive; that he had several plants in his room and had a great desire to buy a sailboat. She had been to his room approximately six times. She never saw a weapon in his room. She noticed that he belittled himself often and wanted to get a graduate degree in psychology but did not feel he could do so. She believes they went to Alpenthal one time and hiked around, SANDY's parents have a condominium at Alpenthal. They would usually go places for one day at a time, never overnight. SANDY's roommate did not like TED. SANDY was living off Freemont & Evanston N. at the time. She describes TED as being in good physical condition; that he would run often and rode his bike to a lot of places. He also went to the Intramural building a lot. TED did not own a car at the time. TED spoke as an intellectual. SANDY describes his voice as having British overtones. He tried to express himself in very intellectual terms. The last time she saw TED was in Sept. 1972. SANDY left the Seattle area in Feb. 1973 and has been in San Francisco since that time. She also recalled that TED liked to do things that were dangerous because he thought they were fun. During the time they picnicked at the river they went swimming and TED was very much enjoyed dunking her. Sometimes SANDY would notice TED staring at her and noticed he was very friendly to many women. He did not talk about any men in his life unless it was in derogatory manner. He thought his mother was weak and was very concerned for his younger sister. SAM BABRO was TED's supervisor at Harborview Hospital and also a professor at the University of Washington. Approximate time TED and SANDY went out together was between June and September 1972 however, she did not consider him to be a serious boyfriend.

Author's note: This pertains to late 1975 (early to mid-November) to early 1976 (late January), after Bundy had been "unmasked" in Utah and had gone home to Seattle for a couple of months. It was a time, Bundy believed, when he could be back on familiar territory among Liz and friends, and get away from the turmoil of Utah and his upcoming trial for the kidnapping of Carol DaRonch. But things would not be peaceful for Ted, and he'd soon learn that the turmoil would continue.

Also, within the record, if you'll look closely, you'll see instances where an officer will purposely add derogatory comments – no doubt in-house humor- concerning those they had to interview. Perhaps these individuals had gotten under their skin a bit for one reason or another. In any event, it's clear they obviously did not care for them. What is a little surprising is that they wrote it all down, certainly believing such scribbling would never see the light of day. Of course, it's no different than what they were already engaging in verbally face-to-face about these people (in their minds it was funny and a way to get a laugh), but that it actually made it into the written record is a little surprising. From a researcher's standpoint, I'm delighted they did.

SEATTLE POLICE DEPARTMENT MEMORANDUM

TO: All Concerned
FROM: Homicide Unit

SUBJECT: Surveillance of Homicide Suspect

This is to be a 24 hr. surveillance of a possible homicide suspect. He is to be watched as closely as possible. He is not to be arrested or confronted in any way unless he commits some overt act warranting immediate arrest (felony or other dangerous act.) Maintain running log of activity.

The subject of this surveillance is Theodore Bundy, WM 29 5-10 160 med. Bld. Brown, hair short, (mod) curly.

He is staying with friends, Marlin L. and Sheila L. Vortman, they live at 3510 W. Elmore Apt. 202. He is driving their 66 Volkswagen Bug, tan in color, Lic. AQB 894. It has a ski rack on the rear deck and has the left taillight out. The Vortmans have another car, a 70 Toyota 4 dr. Wash. Lic. IIP 828, Mrs. Vortman usually drives this car.

Subject has a girlfriend that he is seeing regularly, she is (redacted), lives at (redacted) 18th NE, apt. is on the first floor, right side of that address. She has an 8 yr. old daughter. Vehicle 66 LT BLUE VOLKSWAGEN WASH. LIC. OPM 001

Another friend that subject has visited recently is Ross Davis, he lives in Federal Way, 29401 9th PL. So.

This surveillance is to be confidential, again no arrest or confrontation is to be contemplated unless absolutely necessary. Keep radio traffic at minimum, do not use subject's name on the air.

Below picture is reasonably recent although his hair is shorter now.

BUNDY'S FRIENDS, ASSOCIATES, AND RESIDENCES THAT HE HAS FREQUENTED AND VEHICLES HE HAS

ACCESS TO:

1. Girlfriend/shack job is (redacted) 18 N.E. lives on ground floor, south side. Has 8 yr. old daughter. Works at University Hospital and usually walks to work. Vehicle Lt. Brown '66 VW Bug OPM 001 and has been parking it in the garage in the alley behind her house.

2. Best friend/bosom buddy Marlin Vortman and wife Sheila Manus live at 2510 W. Elmore St. #202 (upper Northwest Corner) just south of entrance to Discovery park on W. Government Way. Vortman is an attorney in the IMB bldg. Wife is a secretary at the University of Washington. Vehicles Lt. Brown '68 VW Bug AQB 894 left taillight may still be out had a ski rack on rear deck. (Bundy has been driving this vehicle almost exclusively since Thanksgiving) White '70 Toyota 4 door sedan IIP 828 usually driven by Vortman's wife to work. Vortman is a white male 6'1 180# short blond hair pompous ass. Shelia is white and has dark shoulder length hair parted in the middle.

3. Good friend/turd Ross Davis lives at 29401 9 PL. S. (Marine Hills) Wife: Sarah …west of Pac. Hwy S. near S. Dash Pt. Rd. He is the state chairman for the Republican Party with offices at 595 Industry Rd. S. (South center in the Andover Park complex) Vehicles White '73 Datsun Station Wagon JCJ 418. Blue '75 Ford LTD Hdtp "GOP 1"

4. Parents: John and Louise Bundy live at 3214 N. 20 Tacoma

5. Cousin: John Cowell lives at 719 N 3rd #202 Tacoma (corner of 3rd and N. Yakima) Works in Wash. Bldg at S. 11 and Pacific Ave in Tacoma. Vehicle Grey '67 Opel

OYV 149

6. Sister: Linda Bundy lives at 109 S. 5ᵗʰ Tacoma but Bundy hasn't been close to her lately.

7. Lawyer here is John H. Brown in the Public Defender's Office.

8. He has been hanging out at the UW law library located at N.E. 41 and Brooklyn Ave. N.E. but has been told that he is not welcome.

Author's note: The following reports continue to detail the surveillance conducted on Bundy when he returned to Seattle in November 1975, but authorities did not locate their suspect until early December.

TO: Capt. Leitch
FROM: Lt. Parks
SUBJECT: Surveillance

All is well at this time, subject is located and under surveillance. Lt. Holder indicates that the squad can handle without problem until Friday afternoon. His superiors should be aware that the squad is going to handle the job totally to clear him. The whole unit will eventually be involved because of court time days off etc. I took it upon myself to tell them that if any overtime is to be utilized they will get it. Don't forget to get hold of Dale Douglas regarding of our use of their car (intelligence). I hope something good comes of the whole thing.

Phil Killien called, I assured him that the squad was aware of his problem and would keep it in mind.

TO: H/R
FROM: TOS Officers Lewis and Fitch

SUBJECT: Bundy Stake-Out / 12-9-75, 0400hrs to 1200hrs.

0815hrs. Susp. left house with (redacted) daughter and got into his veh. Dropped daughter off at school. Susp. went E/B on NE 52 and lost us in traffic after crossing 15 NE. Search made for veh. Proved negative.

084hrs Susp. observed walking S/B on 19 NE from NE 55. Off. Circled block and lost sight of susp. Most likely went back to house.

0915hrs. Susp's veh. Located 2000block. NE 58. Next to entrance to Ravenna Park.

Author's note: The following is from Seattle PD Officer Terrance D. Augerson, dated 12-5-75:

Our subject gave the w/f a kiss then the w/f gave our subject a big hug. The subject then walked around the north side of the residence with w/f 9 while the w/f 20's departed S/W bound. The subject & the w/f 9 then drove to the front of University Hospital and picked up w/f 20's wearing beige clothing. Subject then drove S/B on I-5 from Montlake to same exit. Subject pulled to curb and we lost him for approximately 3 minutes due to very heavy traffic. I located his veh. parked & unoccupied at Occidental & Wash. Parked at a meter. At approx. 1810 subject returned to his veh. with same two females & drove around downtown. He pulled to curb several times and circled block.

Subject then drove N/B on I-5 to Worth gate and entered shopping mall. Subject accompanied by same two w/f entered his veh….then drove N/B on I-5 to 145th exit. Subject drove to Big Boy Restaurant at 145 & Aurora & parked in rear.

Author's note: The following is the report of Detective Ted Fonis of the Seattle Police Department, dated 10-3-75:

1500 hours: Into office for shift work and conference with Lt. Parkes. While in the office it was later told to me, that a subject by the name of TED BUNDY had been apprehended in the city of Salt Lake City, Utah and was now in confinement at the Salt Lake County Sheriff's jail, and was being held on $100,000.00 Bail charging kidnapping and attempted criminal homicide. Discovered that King County Authorities had knowledge of this and that many factors had transpired. Conference was held by CID Administrators this date, and it has been decided to send two agents from this city and the county to Salt Lake City, Utah. It was decided that this writer would accompany King County Det. Robert Keppel to that city, leaving on October 4, 1975 at 0715 hours via United Airlines.

10-4-75 1115 hours: Arrive Salt Lake City, Utah, called Salt Lake County Sheriff's Office, and talk to Det. Thompson. Traveled to motel and checked in, and met Det. Thompson, where (we had a) lengthy conversation with him on their case involving BUNDY.   From all appearances they have a solid case.

Author's note: Fonis and Keppel were itching to interview Bundy, but Thompson informed them that as Bundy made bail, his attorney, John O'Connell, petitioned the judge "that NO ONE, NO ONE, BE ALLOWED TO CONVERSE WITH HIS CLIENT," and the judge granted it. They also wanted to view Bundy's murder kit, "real evidence" as they called it, but were prevented from this because the evidence room guy, who had the key, was not working that day and was out hunting. However, Fonis, Keppel, and Thompson would have a very productive day going over case files and discussing the murders in Washington, Utah, and Colorado. Here is that portion of the report:

10-4-75 continued: After lengthy discussion of the homicides in their area and also of the State of Colorado, Det. Thompson drove us to MURRAY, Utah, where their case was explained in detail, showing the area of actual incident, and also path of travel used in the kidnapping and assault. This entire episode is on their report, statements etc., which are contained in files, our city. On their homicide at Bountiful, Utah, and in Colorado, we are shown photographs of their victims. All are NUDE, and one shows a piece of nylon around the throat, with a set of beads attached to the string. We are told that there were two strands of beads around victim's neck, and only ONE IS LEFT ON victim's neck. The area of the head is brutally assaulted and one point's similarity to the remains found at Taylor Mt. We request copies of their autopsy reports and all reports pertaining to their homicides (in) their area. Det. Thompson stated that they have pieces of evidence such as handcuffs and other items that they have sent to FBI lab for tests. He will inform us of the results.

December 5, 1975 Seattle PD report by Phil G. Allen:

12-5-75 at 1220 hours, on post. According to predecessors, subject is in the house and the car is in the garage at location #2.

1630 hours Subject and small W-F left the house in ABQ 894, drove to U of W Hospital. There he picked up W-F. went southbound south bound on I-5 into Pioneer Square. Tried to lose us and was successful. Officer Augerson found car parked in the 100 blk S. Washington a short time later unoccupied.

1809 hours- Subject and both females returned to the car

walking south-bound from Yesler on Occidental Ave S. drove uptown on third Ave, tried to lose us around 6th and 7th Pike and Olive – unsuccessful. Subject would pull to the curb and turn out his lights, then pull away again. Subject got on the freeway northbound and drove to Northgate arriving there at 1830 hours. They parked in the lot south of 103rd and entered the complex – did not follow.

1930 - Subject, girlfriend and the little girl came out of Northgate complex and entered their vehicle. They drove back to I-5 and went northbound to 145th, where they exited and went over to Aurora Stopped at JB's hamburger restaurant.

1955- Subject still inside when relief arrives T. Blair and G. Olsen

1/12/76 – Bundy in the area of 47th and 16th N.E. He just disappeared.

2128 hrs. – Notified by Det. GILLIS that Bundy had returned to the residence.

2135 hrs. – Bundy went out the front of the house. He approached Det. GILLIS, who was parked on the southwest corner of the intersection of 18th and 52nd. He took GILLIS' picture. He then walked down towards the alley where I'm parked and come up to the front of the car and bent down to where he could see my license plate, and he wrote my license number down. He then walked south back through the alley up to 52nd. I got out on foot and followed him. He stopped at the corner and started talking to Det. GILLIS, who by this time was out on foot. At this time I then approached BUNDY, and we all three talked for a little bit. He wanted to know why we were following him, what took us so long – he's been in town a week. He said he tried to get a hold of

Capt. LEITCH and Capt. MACKIE to find out why, and he said he didn't have any beef with the guys out on the street, and he said he might have to go back to court on the 20th of this month – he doesn't know yet, but he says definitely, for sure, on the 9th of February. We talked for approximately 10 minutes, and about 2145 hrs he went back in to the residence. TED was wearing a blue nylon down jacket, light tan corduroy pants, brown shoes, no hat, and he had about a month's growth of beard; he had it shaved, the neck part, the beard was on his chin and his side burn area, but under the neck was trimmed. It looked about a month's growth.

Some additional comments that TED made during the conversation – he was wondering how much money the county was going to spend watching him and how long we were going to do it, and he made the comment why weren't we out catching the bombers or the weatherman or the radicals, and he also stated that there was really nothing he could do because we weren't breaking any law watching him, but at times, he wanted to be with people and he wanted some privacy.

12-8-75 hrs. Det's. Sutlovich and Ahl relieved other surveillance units at location #2 (5208 18th Ave NE) *Author's note: This was Liz Kloepfer's actual address, mistakenly not redacted.*

1600 hrs. Subject came out of door of loc #2, emptied the garbage and waved at Sutlovich, then walked to the surveillance vehicle and asked if Sutlovich was a police officer, at the same time stating that the vehicle that Sutlovich was in was the same one that followed him last Saturday night. He got no real reply and then continued passing the time of day with small talk, then went back to residence. He was wearing a long sleeved turtleneck sweater and jeans.

1607 hrs. Subject came back out of Loc #2 wearing also a blue jacket and glasses. He walked over again to Sutlovich and stated that he was going to pick up his laundry, Sutlovich followed him to a cleaners at approx 42 NE and University Way, then back to Location #2. Arrived back at 1700 hrs.

1700 hrs. Subject contacted Sutlovich again and asked if the surveillance was for his protection. Sutlovich informed him that he could consider it that. He then stated that's good, that he doesn't have anything against the police, that he was wondering why the surveillance just started since he came back to town a week ago. Sutlovich then asked him if he would be going anywhere soon. He asked "You mean back to Utah". Sutlovich said no, tonight. He stated that he may be going over to Vortmans in Magnolia, then walked back to Location #2 and entered.

1755 hrs. Subject came out of Loc #2 alone and drove crème VW AQB 894 to the Campus Ice Creamery and Grocery at 50th NE and 12th. He came out with a bag of groceries and drove back to the residence.

1920 hrs. Subject, girlfriend and her daughter left Loc #2 in grn VW AMP 001 went to University Village, went Xmas tree shopping.

1945 hrs. After picking out tree, drove to Ernst Hardware at University village, with tree on car.

2005 hrs. Exited store, drove home (Loc#2) arrived there about 2015 hrs.

2015 hrs. Sutlovich relieved by Det. A. Sorenson. END OF SHIFT.

Author's note: What follows is a brief statement given by

Marilyn Hammond to king County Detective Kathleen McChesney on October 7, 1975:

Marilyn Hammond, Rt 3 Box 40, Olympia, Washington 98506

Occupation & Employer: Senate Republican Caucus

I remember meeting Ted Bundy during the summer of 1973, right after I began working for the Senate Republican Caucus. I only knew him on a business basis. He'd sit around in the caucus room and talk with people and I'd talk with him then. I recall on one occasion seeing Ted with a cast or a bandage on one of his forearms-I don't remember which arm. I am not sure if the time I saw this bandage or cast was in the summer of 1973 or 1974. I recall seeing him one time during the summer of 1974 so this could have been the time I saw the bandage or cast. I did not ask Ted what happened to his arm. I have read the above and it is true and correct to the best of my knowledge and memory.

Marilyn Hammond

Author's note: The following Seattle police report discusses Bundy and his attorneys, John Browne in Seattle and John O'Connell in Salt Lake City, and the overall aspects of how the Seattle authorities were going to put pressure on Bundy while he was home in Seattle. It also shows Bundy's clear frustration at being tracked by the police, and his complete inability to do anything about it.

12-1-75 1435 hrs. Request to call Killien. Called Killien. He wants Mackie and Leitch to meet with Boerner to discuss what we are going to do and say in our community re Bundy and his return to the University District. (Killien was the first one to notify me that Bundy was back in town).

12-1-75 1600 hrs. Mackie called and states they heard from a friend of (redacted, but this will be girlfriend Liz) that Bundy was back in the area on Thanksgiving. Mackie just learned this this A.M, Mackie says detectives have been looking for Bundy but have not located him. (Redacted – Liz) is no longer cooperative and is now on Bundy's side. Mackie and Keppel will attend meeting with Boerner at 10 A.M. on 12-2-75.

12-2-75 hrs. Met with Boerner, Killien, Mackie, Keppel, Moore and Leitch. Mackie and Keppel briefed Boerner on a day by day case by case basis of all the information they had on Bundy that would implicate him in 15 minutes. Killien discussed the fact that each of the involved prosecutors had agreed to collectively negotiate a plea-bargain with Bundy's attorney, O'Connell and that O'Connell had been approached and also advised of some of the circumstantial evidence the police had on the multistate murders. O'Connell is a good straight attorney with a job to do but he is receptive to discussing certain matters with the police. John Henry Brown of the Public Defender's Office is representing Bundy on any problems in this area and Brown has the reputation for being totally uncooperative and a crusader.

12-2-75 Mackie relates that Bundy showed up at Horatio's Restaurant, (11-27-75) where (redacted – Liz) was having dinner with some friends. He wanted (redacted) to leave with him but she refused but did meet him at her place later that night.

12-2-75 1300 hrs. Bundy was seen at the University of Washington Law School by two people that know him personally. Some kind of incident occurred and he left.

Author's note: What follows is, I believe, the accurate time

Bundy spent with Ann Rule during their luncheon that day. In her book, Rule states the meeting lasted three hours, but the police record states two hours and 15 minutes. In my opinion, it is a simple mistake on the part of Rule, as the police were actively tracking Bundy and were accurately recording their time and locations while Bundy was under surveillance.

12-2-75 1400 Hrs. – 1615 Hrs. He had lunch with Ann Rule at the Pittsbourg, etc. in Pioneer Square. He did not say anything incriminating, was totally relaxed but did ask a lot of questions about what was going on here and stated he wanted to talk to the police.

12-5-75 0900 hrs. Sgt. Jack Moore states that his son Scott who works in the Safeway Store at 50th and Brok. had Bundy as a customer at about 2115 hrs. on 12-4-75. Scott knows Bundy personally and states they had a short conversation. And that Bundy bought a bottle of wine and left. Sgt. Moore will submit the contents of the conversation on Monday. Bundy was wearing a heavy Indian type sweater and cloth belt. (Leitch)

Author's note: The following report, dated 11-7-75, comes from the files of Detective Rodger Dunn (Bob Keppel's partner), pertaining to Ted Bundy's interactions with Ross Davis and his activities with the Washington State Republican Party.

1040 hrs. Contacted Ross E. Davis at Republican Headquarters, 595 Industry Dr. S., Tukwila

[Ross Davis] who first met Bundy around March, 1973, and was immediately impressed by the guy. Bundy began working at the headquarters in Olympia on a part-time basis in April, 1973, and then was elevated to Davis' assistant wherein he had expenses paid access to credit cards and stood I for him on one occasion. *(Author's note: Obvious mistakes here leaving the meaning of the writer unclear.)* He and Bundy because close personal and professional friends and he would come to their home in Olympia weekly for dinner, to take the dog for a walk and play with the kids. His wife Sarah really thought highly of Bundy and was upset by the arrest in Utah.

Bundy introduced him to (redacted) in September, 1973, and had dinner at his house. They then borrowed the leased car that Davis drove for the party: Blue/White '73 Ford LTD 2dr. Wn. PL. BTR 416 and drove to a condominium at Alpenthal with (redacted) Davis said he did not know who the condo belonged to but said it was not his or the Republican party's.

(Author's note: 'Redacted' refers to Bundy's girlfriend, identified in my first book as Carla Browning from San Francisco, and Ross Davis confirmed this when we spoke by phone during my research for The Bundy Murders *in 2007. Davis also said that Ted never mentioned the name Liz Kloepfer to him)*

Davis got the impression that Ted loved (redacted) a lot and expected them to get married. He didn't know of any other girls Bundy was dating.

They moved the Headquarters office from 497 Tyree Dr. Olympia to the Southcenter office on 8-30-73.

Davis said that Bundy didn't abuse any drugs. He saw him high at parties but never bombed. Bundy occasionally took No-Doze to stay awake and would work all night at the office. Bundy attended meetings at a high level with Davis but was not one of the strategists of the party during 1973. Sometime around the end of January, 1974, Davis saw

Bundy at a work party for a legislative candidate. He was doing volunteer work. Bundy mentioned that he had broken up with (*redacted – Carla Browning*) but didn't appear to be depressed by it. (*Author's note: He wasn't upset at all, as it was payback for Carla breaking up with him previously.*)

Davis never noticed anything about Bundy's behavior that appeared deviant, and said that he contributed to the defense fund and probably will contribute more in the future. Davis has not spoken to Bundy since he was charged in Utah and said that the last time he talked to him was about six months ago when he called from Utah and they talked for a half an hour. Bundy mentioned the burglary tools arrest in passing and said there wasn't much to it. I told Davis what the burglary tools consisted of, and he said that he often saw a ski mask in Bundy's car since he was a skier, and he had to carry tools to work on his VW (ice pick and crowbar), and he had rebuilt his VW from other car's parts, the rope was there to tow his car, and Davis had to give him a tow off the freeway one time because his distributor had conked out. And Davis had seen handcuffs in Bundy's car in the past but didn't know why he carried them around.

On 4-18-73 an application for a nationwide credit account was filled out by the Republican State Central Committee. They requested two cards and the only authorized card holders were to be "R.E. Davis" and "T.R. Bundy". The cards were granted under account ..... Under bank references, the party listed accounts with Seattle-First National Bank / Olympia Branch and Puget Sound National Bank / Tacoma Branch.

Bundy also had access to a "Select Credit Card" issued to the party under account .... The billings from the company were badly past due and there were only three people's initials on charges during May, June, and July, 1973: TB, RED, MHA.

Author's note: What follows is a partial list of charges Bundy made on the Select card for the listed months of 1973:

Between 4-23-73 and 7-10-73, Bundy ate 18 times at the Tyee Restaurant in Olympia; he ate at Gasperetti's in Seattle on 5-8-73; the Davenport Hotel in Spokane on 5-17-73; and University Towers on 6-29-73.)

Author's note: What follows is from the report of Det. Roger Dunn, recording a conversation he had with Frank Morris, dated 11-10-75

1500 hrs. Frank Morris called the office to say he first met Bundy during the '72 elections when Bundy was working on the Evans campaign and he was working on the Lud Kramer campaign. He thought (Bundy) was a handsome guy who would have no trouble getting dates with girls and never noticed anything out of the ordinary. Morris succeeded Bundy as Davis' assistant when he left to go to law school and that was the last time he saw him. Morris offered an explanation that I had never heard concerning Bundy. He kept referring to all of the cases as "sex crimes" and that if Bundy were involved it would be because Bundy could not get off through straight sex and had to get into perversions to get satisfied.

Author's note: The following account of the "cat and mouse" chase of Bundy around the university district by Roger Dunn and Bob Keppel, is dated 1-13-76, and shows clearly how much Bundy wanted to get away from his pursuers. Bundy had been at Liz's apartment, and the chase began there. Bundy kept the detectives active the entire day.

0825 hrs. Bundy came out the front door and began walking south on 18 N.E. He had on dark rimmed glasses, blue down ski parka, tan flared trousers, dark shoes and was carrying a green satchel under his left arm. He had about a month's growth of beard and moustache. I got out of my car and followed him on foot after advising Keppel.

Bundy walked at a normal pace up to 17. N.E. and south into the campus and was aware that I was behind him. He walked in near the Burke Museum and then back out onto 45th. He turned south on University Way N.E. very aware that I was behind him.

With hope gone of a covert tail, I decided to make an overt tail to gauge Bundy's reactions. So I closed the interval to 20'.

0840 hrs. He went into the Coffee Corral at N.E. 42 and U Way and came out a moment later smoking a cigarette.

0844 hrs. He went into the office of Student Affairs at N.E. 41 and U Way and walked into room 170 A and inquired about a $1000 loan. I positioned myself in the corridor so he would walk by me but as he exited, he only looked at me and didn't make any effort to speak or acknowledge that I was there staring at him.

0846 hrs. He came out of the building and walked back into campus. As we waited at the light at N.E. 41 and 15 N.E. I positioned myself directly behind him at the interval of 2' but he still did not acknowledge me.

0850 hrs. He walked up through Red Square and into the undergraduate library. As we got into a crowd, he went downstairs and through the cafeteria in an effort to lose me.

0855 hrs. Bundy went into a phone booth in Suzallo Library. The portion of the conversation I could hear was "There's a detective following me, where's the car?"

0858 hrs. Bundy came out of the phone booth and went into the men's room P 36A in Suzallo Library. I paused a moment to catch up on my notes thinking that the restrooms had only one entrance.

0901 hrs. I went into the restroom and discovered that there was a backdoor that opened into an employees' locker room and an adjoining stairway to the scientific stacks. I checked for Bundy in the immediate area but he was gone.

0915 hrs. I checked the Psych. Dept. in Guthrie Hall to see if he may have been en route to talk with Dr. Elizabeth Loftus but he was not around.

0920 hrs. Called Keppel and advised that Bundy was lost and that he may be headed for (redacted – but Liz)'s car which Keppel had located near N.E. Boat and 15th N.E.

0940 hrs. I walked back to my vehicle where det. Strunk and Eblin were driving past. I advised them what Bundy was wearing in case they spotted him.

0950 hrs. I drove to the UW Law Library at N.E. 41 and 12 N.E. and checked from top to bottom without luck.

1015 hrs. Guthrie Hall again, nothing.

1030 hrs. Student Union Building and Lounges, nothing.

1050 hrs. Suzallo Library, nothing.

1130 hrs. Administration Building, nothing.

1200 hrs. Called Sgt. Lettich and advised of the status.

1230 hrs. I drove to Marlin Vortman's apartment in an effort to relocate Bundy. As I approached the apartment I spotted Bundy walking along the sidewalk dressed in a grey hooded sweatshirt, faded green sweatpants, blue turtleneck and white tennis shoes. When he saw me he smiled. I waved and continued past him to the corner of 36 W. And W. Gov't Way. As I turned south I looked in my rearview mirror and saw Bundy sprinting into the woods in Discovery Park. It was raining moderately at the time.

1233 hrs. The district S.P.D. patrol car came by and I advised the officer (badge # 284) that Bundy was in the area. He said he would advise military police and the horse patrol that was in the park.

1245 hrs. I contacted the cleaners on the corner near the Vortman's apartment, but Bundy had not been in. Vortman was a frequent customer, but he had not been in recently.

1255 hrs. I parked in the parking lot south of the apartment house and Bundy came walking back and entered the door on the west end.

1257 hrs. Bundy came out of the east door still dressed in the sweats and smoking a cigarette. He walked between the apartment and out of sight toward the front of the apartment. I waited a moment and then decided to drive around the area to see if Bundy had another car stashed that he could have driven to the area in since Keppel was still sitting on (redacted- but Liz)'s car.

1308 hrs. I spotted Bundy walking up to Vortman's tan VW AQB 894 parked on W. Thurman near 34 W. When he saw me, he continued walking past the vehicle and walked down through the ravine on the east side of Vortman's apartment so I couldn't follow him in my vehicle. I felt like Bundy would return to the VW so I returned to it and waited.

1328 hrs. Bundy walked up the street to the vehicle. It

apparently didn't start so he had to push it and then went to Gov't Way. Down through Fisherman's Terminal and north on 15 N.W. toward Ballard.

I followed Bundy down into Ballard's business district and it soon became evident that the only reason he was driving at all was to play tag with the cops. He would drive legally but try his best to lose me. Some typical maneuvers would be: park the car in hopes that I would have to drive by in traffic and or get out of the car (in sweats) and walk down the block, walk down the block, get one car between us at a stoplight and then make a free right turn and then a few more turns in an effort to get free of a tail. It became very easy to predict what Bundy would try to do but my car was not conducive to quick albeit legal maneuvers. Bundy was taking great delight in the 'game' and smiled when he would execute a clever evasive tactic.

1407 hrs. Bundy drove to the Ballard Locks, parked his car and jogged (in heavy rain) back along the railroad tracks and out of sight around the end of the government property.

Since Bundy's behavior had become predictable, I parked my car next to his and waited. 1416 hrs. Bundy came walking back to the car from the same direction. I got two impressions as to why Bundy uses a tactic of parking the car and walking away:

1. He hoped that I would immobilize the operation of the car so he could scream 'harassment'.

2. Hoped that I would get out and follow him on foot so he could double back to the car so he could drive off without a tail.

1419 hrs. Bundy made a free right turn at the light at 15

N.W. and Market and I was boxed in and couldn't follow.

1423 hrs. I believe Bundy continued south on 15 N.W. and made it across the bridge before it opened. I didn't however, and Bundy was lost.

1435 hrs. I checked around Vortman's apartment for the vehicle, but couldn't find it.

1437 hrs. I got a message from radio via Sgt. Nolan to discontinue to attempt to locate Bundy and return to the office.

My impressions of Bundy during the day while I was following him is that he does not act like a normal, mature 29 year old law student. He seems to thrive on attention just like a spoiled child and that is the only reason he altered his behavior, which is to say the more 'attention' he gets, the more he eats it up. It would not be difficult to predict his actions in a situation like this, but trying to maintain a covert surveillance in hopes that he may go to a 'stash' or any other place that might tend to incriminate him would be fruitless and impractical.

Det. Keppel and I reviewed the day's activities with Capt. Mackie and he made a decision to conduct a periodic spot check on Bundy with whoever may be in the area with some spare time. S.P.D. will take the same policy.

Author's note: On August 19, 1974, Ted Bundy paid $19 to Pande-Cameron located at 815 Pine Street in Seattle, for the washing and repairing of an Oriental rug. Besides the cleaning, the invoice notes charges were for the sewing and patching of two splits.

Author's note: The following information has to do with the interview of a potential Bundy victim, Jacqueline (or Jackie) Plishkie, and the encounter she believed to have had with Bundy at Lake Sammamish. Plishkie rode her bike to the lake that hot Sunday afternoon, and entered the park around 4:00 p.m. As she parked her bike in the designated area, she noticed a man with a sling on his left arm who was staring at her. Plishkie, as she remembered it, was wearing "blue jeans, sort of cut-offs, and a pink, very brief bikini top." About fifteen minutes later, as she watched the water skiers at the jumping off point, Bundy approached her (which must mean he was trailing her the entire time), and asked for help so that he could get his sailboat loaded onto his car. Plishkie told the man she wasn't very strong, to which Bundy responded "It's better that I asked someone who was alone." She then informed him she was waiting for someone, and with that, Bundy blurted out, "Oh, I see!" and walked off. It was now 4:20 p.m., and within minutes, Bundy would stop and convince Denise Naslund to leave with him, after he spotted her walking out of the restroom at the far end of the park. What follows is a report from King County Police Department dated September 3, 1975, fourteen months after the incident.

9-3-75 1030 hrs … photos were shown to JACKIE PLISHKIE who pulled out TED's photograph and held it in her hand, she stated she did not know why she took out that particular photograph, she did not pull out any other photograph. (*Author's note: Plishkie would tell detectives a month later that she had seen some photos of Bundy published in the local newspapers after his arrest.*)

10-7-75 1715 hrs. Contacted Scott Flegal … and received a group of ski lift tickets that he had saved. He had gone skiing with Chris and Bundy at Crystal Mtn. during the fall of 1973 or winter of early 1974. He couldn't recall the exact date but it is represented by one of the lift tickets. He said that on that occasion, Bundy fell on his ski and got a bloody nose. He doesn't recall him going to the aid station but he got pretty tired and slept in the backseat all the way home. His impression was that it was about Christmas 1973.

10-13-75 The A.P.B. sent out on Bundy was released via the AP wire service and the Tacoma News Tribune printed the phrase about Bundy being a "prime suspect." The paper was placed in file.

Author's note: The following report is from the Colorado authorities and pertains to the murder of Caryn Campbell.

CARYN CAMPBELL

Age: 23

Description: 5'5", 112 pounds,

Long brown hair parted in the middle, brown eyes

White Female

Registered Nurse

Last seen wearing: an off-white or beige colored coat, about mid-length, with fur on the collar and down the front and around the cuffs; a black pullover sweater with flowers on it; blue jeans with bell bottoms; black rough-out boots, size: wore a 34C bra, clothing 9 or 10 in size.

The subject turned up missing on January 12, 1975, at approximately 8:00 p.m. from the Wildwood Inn in Aspen, Colorado, and her completely nude body was found February 17, 1975, at approximately 2.8 miles up the canyon from the lodge where she disappeared from.

The subject had apparently been taken and dumped off the side of the canyon road in the snow. The body had apparently been there for about 37 days covered in snow. The coyotes apparently pulled the body out from under the snow and had been chewing on it when it was located. Because the neck and part of the head had been completely chewed away by the animals, it is unknown whether the girl was strangled or not. She did appear to have bruises, contusions, and lacerations, etc., and also on the back of the head she had two or three lacerations, which appear to be the same type as the two girls had in the Utah area. The back of the skull had also been fractured, but due to the decomposition, and the animal chewing on the body, the Medical Examiner could not give an exact cause of death. Background on this girl, she came from Detroit, Michigan, the night before she turned up missing, with a doctor who she had been living with for the past year. She was last seen getting off an elevator in the Wildwood Lodge, was going back to her room to pick up a magazine and go back downstairs to the lounge area, and apparently never made it to the room. That was the last she was heard from or seen. She had also just come from a dinner at the Stew Pot at the lodge and had a stew dinner. According to the Medical Examiner, the stew was still in her stomach and had not yet digested.

Author's note: The following report is pertaining to Sandra Jean Weaver, a possible (I want to say probable, as there are more than a few similarities between Bundy's known murders and this one) Bundy victim who disappeared from Salt Lake City, Utah, on July 1, 1974. Her body was recovered in Colorado.

SANDRA JEAN WEAVER

DOB: 8-4-55

Description: White female, 5'7", 120 lbs.

Long brown hair parted in the middle, blue eyes.

Last believed to be wearing: Blue pants, possibly Levis or corduroy; the rest of the clothing is unknown.

The subject was missing on 7-1-74 at approximately 10:00 a.m. from the Wycoff Building in Salt Lake City, Utah; was found completely nude on 7-2-74 at 4:00 p.m. in Grand Junction, Colorado.

This subject was found dumped off a canyon road at Palisades Canyon in Colorado. Her body was just a short distance from the Colorado River. The only piece of clothing found on her was a necklace, which she had been known to be wearing when last seen. This girl also appeared to have been dumped off from the top of the canyon road down, as there was no indication of any footprints or any drag marks whatsoever, according to Colorado authorities. According to Colorado Medical Examiner, he believes that she had had sexual intercourse previous to her death. She had also been strangled, possibly with hands or an object, it is unknown what. She also had numerous bruises, contusions, etc. on her back and around her head, however, apparently not as severe as Melissa Smith or Laura Aime. A background on this individual, she left La Crosse, Wisconsin, in June with another girlfriend and a boy hitchhiking their way to Salt Lake. They arrived in the Salt Lake area and then went to Tooele, where they were living with a couple of boys in a trailer in Tooele. They obtained a job at Wycoff in Salt Lake City. The two girls hitchhiked back and forth continually. The victim was known to use drugs extremely heavily, and also had gone to bed with numerous boys in the area. In fact, her boyfriend, the night she left before she was missing, admitted to having sexual intercourse with her at that time. On July 1, 1974, she was taken by two individuals and dropped off at the Wycoff Building in Salt Lake at approximately 8:00 a.m. She was observed leaving the job by a couple of individuals between 10:00 and 11:00 a.m. that date, and was never seen or heard from since. According to her girlfriend and the boys in the Tooele area, she never got back to the trailer that day. However, her body was never identified until January of 1975. This girl, the same as the others, apparently had been killed somewhere else and dumped in this area here again. No clothing has ever been found, and according to Colorado, they have a few hair fibers that were on the body. This is the only evidence that Colorado has. She also had long fingernails apparently just freshly manicured not too long ago.

Author's note: The following report is from the files of Detective Ira Beal of Bountiful, Utah. It's dated September 19, 1975, and it pertains to Mary Lynn Chino and her Seattle connection to Ted Bundy. Chino is most likely the "Angie" spoken of in Liz Kendall's The Phantom Prince. Once again, "redacted" will appear, and, once again, it pertains to Liz.

Complainant: Dean Kent
Victim: Debra Kent

This is an interview of Mary Lynn Chino, 914 Emerson, Seattle, Washington.

Mary was asked how long she had known Ted and she stated she had known him for approximately six years, that she was with (redacted) when they met Ted at a bar approximately six years ago.

Mary was then asked how well she knew Ted. She stated she knew more about Ted from her conversations with (redacted), however, she has from time to time had some in-depth conversations with Ted. She did not elaborate as to what they were about.

Mary was then asked how old she would guess Ted was. She stated she did not know his exact age, however, she would guess he was approximately 25 years of age. She then stated she noticed how he has aged considerably in the last year but previous to that he looked much younger.

Mary stated that she had never started thinking about Ted in relation to possibly being the one involved in the disappearances of the girls in the Seattle area until (redacted) approached her. She stated this was in July of 1974. She stated at that time (redacted) came to her apartment with the composite stating that someone at work had stated, ha, is this your boyfriend. She stated at that time they started trying to link things together. At that time, the girl who disappeared on July 14th of 1974 had just disappeared from the Lake State Park and the description fit Ted exactly, especially the clothes he was wearing as Ted dressed exactly that way.

Mary stated that in October she came to Utah to visit her parents in Ogden. At that time she discovered the disappearance of the girl in Salt Lake, this being Melissa Smith, and upon her return to Seattle she contacted (redacted) and told her about the girl missing in Salt Lake being very similar to the ones that had turned up missing in the Seattle area.

Mary then left and went to Europe and did not return to Seattle until December. Mary was then asked if she observed any unusual things or any unusual actions in Ted's actions. She stated one night she was out late, coming home approximately 2:00 a.m. and as she entered her house, she observed Ted out walking in the yards behind her house. This is in the University District near the area where Ted was living. She stated this occurred in 1972 and she feels he was stealing at this time. Mary was then asked if she recalled a ripped seat in Ted's car and she stated she did not remember it.

Mary was then asked if Ted ever made any comments to her regarding the missing girls in the Seattle area and she stated he had not. Mary was asked if Ted had ever made any advances toward her sexually and she stated he had not. Mary was then asked if she knew when (redacted) talked with the police. She stated she did and (redacted) had talked with her just prior to going to the police and in fact she had kind of encouraged (redacted) to go.

Mary was then asked if she had any ideas as to what type of hairdos Ted liked or any particular style or type of girl that he liked. She stated he loved long hair and liked to play with (redacted)'s hair all the time, always running his fingers and hands through it.

Mary was then asked if she knew of any of Ted's friends. She stated Ted did not have many friends in Seattle. The people she knew that had met Ted saw through him as a phony. Mary was then asked if it would be hard for Ted to start a conversation with a stranger such as picking up a girl. She stated this would be very easy for him to do this as he dressed very well, was a good conversationalist and was very good looking and it would be very easy to strike up a conversation with a strange girl and possibly talk her into going with him. Mary was then asked if Ted had ever said anything to her or around her in regards to evidence or laws of evidence regarding his work or schooling as an attorney. She stated he had not.

Mary then stated that Ted calls all the time from Salt Lake and whenever she is at (redacted)'s apartment and he calls and (redacted) is not at home he gets quite upset. She also stated that if Ted calls and no one is home at (redacted)'s apartment he will immediately call her apartment and be very upset because (redacted) is not at home. She stated he is very jealous of (redacted).

Mary was then asked if she knew how Ted was getting his money for his schooling. She stated Ted did not come from a rich family, he did not have very much money. She stated she is sure he steals things to get money, that he lies. She stated she knows he has lied to her and he has also lied to (redacted). Mary went on to state that one time when they were taking a river trip, that he likes to get down the river into the rapids area and go further than he should deliberately to try and scare the girls that are with him as he just loves to see girls scared.

Mary was then asked if she knew Ted owned a gun. She stated she did not know.

This completes the interview with Mary Chino.

(Author's note: What follows is the testimony of Thomas Sampson, a coworker of Ted Bundy. The two men had an opportunity to work together at two Washington State agencies, and they socialized together on occasion. It's clear from his testimony that he liked Bundy, and did not see anything unusual about him.)

Statement of:

Thomas Gregory Sampson

I do hereby give the following statement to Paul Barclift, whom I know to be a Deputy Sheriff of Thurston County, Washington, as an aid to investigation, and all facts contained herein are true to the best of my knowledge and belief.

Q. Mr. Sampson, are you acquainted with Theodore R. Bundy?

A. Yes, I am.

Q. Where did you first meet Mr. Bundy?

A. I first met Ted Bundy in 1972, when he applied for a job with the Seattle Crime Prevention Commission. I worked with him with the Crime Prevention Commission and also at Emergency Services in 1974.

Q. While you were in Seattle, what was your relationship with him?

A. Ted Bundy was Assistant Director of the Seattle Crime Prevention Commission and I was the Director of the Seattle Crime Prevention Commission in 1972. I hired Ted Bundy on the recommendation of Donna Shram of the Law and Justice Planning Office in Seattle. In Olympia, we were simply co-workers in the Department of Emergency Services and off the job, we were friends, and ate together infrequently and played racket ball (sic).

Q. How would you describe Mr. Bundy?

A. Ted was well-behaved, well-dressed, intelligent, and acted extremely proper at all times. He was an aggressive, hardnosed individual, who was a competent, hardworking, good writer, and extremely valuable in his public relation functions and always did his job well and on time.

Q. Were you aware of the project that Bundy worked on referenced rapes, hitchhiking, and assaults while he was with the Seattle Crime Commission?

A. Yes, Ted did a job for us on assaults on women while he was with the Crime Prevention Commission and published a very short article in our December Crime Commission bulletin.

Q. Do you have any knowledge of where the files and records are at this time?

A. No, I don't, but I don't believe Ted Bundy would have taken them.

Q. Prior to the time that he began to work for the Department of Emergency Services, did you ever see him or know him to be out at the Evergreen College Campus grounds?

A. We played racket ball (sic) at Evergreen State College on one occasion I seem to recall, but not positively, him playing racket ball (sic) there at other times. We may have played more than once there at the colleges.

Q. Now, was this during the time he was employed by Department of Emergency Services or prior to that?

A. That is correct. It was during the Emergency Services employment. It would be through the end of May and the middle of August.

Q. Did he ever visit you at your residence at 3808 Country Club Drive?

A. He may have, on one occasion, visited me there at the

house.

Q. Did you ever see Bundy wearing a cast or having his arm in a sling?

A. I don't recall.

Q. You stated previously that while he was working for Department of Emergency Services that you, infrequently, went with him to eat. What establishment did you patronize?

A. Richard's Round House and locations which were near the Emergency Services office.

Q. You also mentioned previously that you had played racket ball (sic) at Evergreen College with Mr. Bundy. Was he proficient in this sport?

A. Darn good, he was. Ted was naturally athletic and he participated in a number of sporting activities. He expressed an interest in taking karate and was a physical individual. I don't know anyone else he might have played racket ball (sic) with at any other time.

Q. To your knowledge, did he attend the Energy Conference that you conducted at Evergreen State College on March 1, 1974?

A. No, he did not.

Q. Do you have any knowledge if Bundy ever went to Oregon?

A. I would not know.

Q. Do you know if he ever stayed with anyone overnight in the Olympia area or at any of the hotels or motels?

A. I seem to recall him mentioning that he did; however, I would not know with whom or when.

Q. Do you know of any friends or acquaintances of Bundy that may have been attending the Evergreen College in March 1974?

A. The only individuals I would be aware of would be the people that might work at the Evergreen State College, students and graduates who worked at the Department of Emergency Services.

Q. Do you know of any reason that Bundy may have gone to the Evergreen State College, during this period, March 1974?

A. No, I don't.

Q. Did you ever have any reason to suspect that Bundy might be "gay"?

A. No.

Q. Do you know what type of vehicle Mr. Bundy drove?

A. A Volkswagen. I'm not sure of the color. I seem to recall it being white, but I can't remember for sure.

Q. Did you ever see him drive any other vehicles?

A. No, I don't think so.

Q. Do you know of anyone in the Olympia area that you would consider a close friend of Bundy?

A. No.

Author's note: What follows are reports from the case file of Georgann Hawkins who was abducted by Ted Bundy on

June 11, 1974. I wrote about Georgann in my first book, <u>The Bundy Murders: A Comprehensive History</u>. Having written about it extensively in that book, I will only be adding that which I did not use that first time around. While the following letter, written by Georgann's father and signed, W. B. Hawkins, did not make it into the first book, I will add it here. The letter is dated July 18th, but is without a year. That year, of course, was 1974. It is also interesting to note that Warren Hawkins had correctly reasoned that there was, in fact, a connection between his daughter's abduction and the other missing girls of Washington State. He also came to the right conclusion as to how the killer abducted her.

The alley behind Greek Row where Georgann Hawkins encountered Ted Bundy. As she walked towards her sorority house, located just beyond the elevated walkway, Bundy was coming up the ally towards her. Feigning injury while hobbling on crutches, she helped him carry a briefcase to a deserted parking lot about one block away where his VW was parked

The parking lot, now paved, where Bundy assaulted and abducted Georgann Hawkins

July 18th
Seattle Police; Missing Person's Dept:
Dear Detective Jelberg:

Enclosed are two pieces of clothing and sunglasses of Georgann's. I hope the medium or psychic you are using isn't going solely on scent or odor of this clothing, for you know how girls share their clothing. And we aren't certain that other girls up at the sorority house didn't wear them at one time or another.

You know, I've pretty well resigned myself that Georgann is dead; and it will be only a matter of time until her body is found. Of course, in the meantime, it becomes a mental torture to my wife and I, since we will have to go through her death all over again.

Reading about the manner in which that suspect abducted Janice Ott, I can't help but feel this guy could very well turn out to be the same one that took Georgann. Because there are no clues, it would indicate to me she went willingly to a car; under the "ruse" of a request for help of some kind. Certainly no one would suspect a person with his arm in a sling, or at least one's fears of any foul play would not be aroused by that person only having one arm at liberty; or at least assumed it being in a cast and a sling of some kind. Of course, the victim wouldn't know if the arm was merely wrapped and placed in a sling, or that it might contain a drug or a weapon of some kind.

I sent (redacted) this postures to Holland today, incidentally I had previously anticipated your request along these lines, and sent off photos of all the missing college coeds; to the National Enquirer newspaper-magazine in Florida, a week or so earlier. I directed it to the person who wrote the article; asking for his aid in soliciting him to locate these missing girls; by the same means he described in his article. I didn't think to send any of this information directly to this Gerard Croiset Jr., in Holland, however. Well, between what I send him today, and hopefully what this newspaper might forward, that he'll get the message of the urgency of this matter. I also sent along the article about the two missing girls (with photos) at Lake Sammamish too!

Well, detective, I'm truly appreciative of your interest of Georgann's disappearance and what seems to be a personal attention you are giving this case over above normal. For both our sakes, I just hope it will be of value; surely evil cannot continue to prevail all the time.

Cordially,
W.B. Hawkins

Author's note: What follows is another report that is included in the various reports that make up the Georgann Hawkins case file, and it describes an individual (Bundy) that a Sharon Harrington saw on July 26, 1974. Without question, it's Bundy, and it is somewhat curious that he was working the same ploy he had used (and in the same general area) when he snatched Georgann Hawkins; the only difference here is that he was attempting to abduct in the morning. This Seattle police report will lead off with the comments of the investigator, and follows with Harrington's statement.

DETAILS: Harrington relates that on 7-26-74 at approximately 1130 a.m. she was walking south on 16th. Ave. Northeast; that the man previously described with the leg cast and briefcase was walking west of 50th. That this guy pulled the same trick walking in front of her and dropping the briefcase and looking back at her as if to get her to stop and help him. When she didn't respond he picked up the briefcase and walked west on 50th towards 17th. This description fits the paper articles.

Seattle Police Department

DATE: August 10, 1974
TIME: 1325
PLACE: HOMICIDE OFFICE
STATEMENT: Sharron Harrington, DOB (I have redacted),
5011-17th Avenue N.E. 525-0114

The above is my true name, DOB, present address & phone.

On July 26, 1974, Friday at approx. 1130 a.m., I was walking south on 16th N.E. and 50th to go to the University shopping area, a white man, whom I describe as approx. 5'9", fairly good build, I think his hair was brown, kind of parted in the middle, length just above the collar, brown eyes, no glasses, no unusual markings about his face, wearing blue jeans. 1 leg was long, one was cut off for his cast. This would be his right leg. The cast appeared to be a full cast, going up to his groin area. The above man was using two crutches. He was wearing some type of shirt, I cannot recall the color, but I know he was not wearing any jacket. The above man was carrying a black brief case, more like the old fashion type it wasn't the square type but round on top. This man passed me, and it was then that I noticed he kept dropping his brief case. He would then pick the brief case up, then he would drop it again. I observed him drop his brief case approx. two times.

I would like to state this man and I were walking in different directions on the same side of the avenue. After he dropped the brief case the first time, I turned my head and looked back at him, and seen him smile and I didn't like the way he looked at me. When he smiled, he picked the case up and continued on. I, at this time, was thinking about helping him, but changed my mind. After he picked his case up, he, as mentioned before, dropped it again. He was looking at me as if he wanted me to help him. I noticed his eyes and they appeared very weird. This more or less gave me the creeps, and I began walking up the avenue very fast. I have not seen this man since.

About the cast, it appeared to be fairly new, very white. No words were exchanged. He was (a) very clean cut person.

STATEMENT TAKEN BY: Det. Ted Fonis.

Author's note: The following report contains information on the murder of Laura Ann Aime, including portions of her autopsy report. I have dealt with her abduction and murder in both my first and second books, so this time around I'm only adding the raw reports. If the reader has a fairly good understanding of the facts pertaining to this particular abduction, the following reports will be a good addition to the full understanding – and the stark realities – surrounding the death of Laura Ann Aime. (Author's note: The Laura Ann Aime story can be found in my book, The Bundy Murders: A Comprehensive History, p. 98-99, 113, 143; and in The Trail Of Ted Bundy: Digging Up the Untold Stories, on p. 72-74.)

One last personal note: Long before I decided to write a book about the Ted Bundy murders, I had the opportunity to view the crime scene photos of Laura Aime. These photos are not readily available to the public, and are extremely graphic in nature, especially the close-up of her face and neck in death, the ligature still tightly wrapped around her throat, which left her tongue protruding from her mouth. Of all the pictures, I viewed of her body that day, this is the one that most sticks in my mind. Viewing them, however, is of utmost importance when writing about any true crime case, as you are able to see everything the investigators had to see when they entered the crime scene.

Author's note: The following report is also from Colorado Investigator Michael Fisher's Similar Transactions, but has a specific heading of "No.2". Of course, there must have been an in-house reason for doing this, but it is not explained in the record.

Similar Transactions No. 2

In the state's offer of proof, testimony and exhibits will be introduced indicating the following: Laura Ann Amie was last seen on October 31, 1974, at a Halloween party where she and several friends got together and consumed alcohol. Along towards midnight, Laura Ann Amie indicated that she wished to go downtown to buy a pack of cigarettes. She wanted to hitchhike. One of her friends refused to go down with her. Laura Ann Amie left by herself. That was the last time she was seen. When she left the Halloween party, she was wearing a halter top and blue jeans with patches on the rear. There is no indication whether or not she was wearing shoes at this time. There will be testimony that she was not wearing nylons. Laura had consumed a considerable amount of alcohol and supposedly going to hitchhike down to American Fork. In the middle of November, two of her friends thought they had received a phone call from her.

Laura Ann Aime's body was found Thanksgiving Day, 1974, in American Fork Canyon, Utah. The area is described as a mountain area. At that time, there was no snow on the ground; but it was completely frozen and covered with leaves. American Fork Canyon is a recreational area with a lot of brush and trees in the area. When the body was found, it was completely nude with the exception of a necklace and a ring with a green stone in it. There was a nylon tightly wrapped around her neck, which had been used as a choking device. Her body was found by a young man and a young lady who were hiding in the area. They saw a light blue Volkswagen in the area at the same time. Laura Ann Amie's body was taken from the scene to the office of the medical examiner where an autopsy was performed at approximately 5:00 p.m. on November 27, 1974.   .

As a general description, the body was that of an unembalmed, well-developed, well-nourished young adult female between 16 and 18 years of age that measures 5'10" in length and weighs about 110 to 120 pounds. The body was naked, and it was covered by multiple leaves, twigs, clusters, and clumps of dirt and caked mud. Scalp hair color is dark brown, 15" to 17" long, parted in the middle, pubic hair is brown. The auxiliary hair had been recently shaved, and the growth of it was less than 1/8"; the eyes were brown, the shoe size was 7E. There was a linear scar on the anterior-lateral aspect of the mid-third of the left forearm that measures ½" in length. This scar is one identifying mark recognized by James Aime, the father of Laura Ann Aime. James Aime identifies the body as that of his daughter, Laura Ann Amie. The autopsy further reveals complexion that is fair to medium with solar hyper pigmentation of the skin of the face, neck, chest, abdomen, upper and lower extremities with areas of non-tanning of the skin in the nape and inter-scapular regions of the back.

There is superficial, irregular, linear abrasion of the skin of the anterior aspect of the neck immediately below the level of the thyroid bone that measures ¾" in length and has a maximum width of 1/8". There (are) irregular, bloodless abrasions of the left pectoral region immediately below the breast, the anterior – lateral aspect of the right hemi thorax and inner aspect of the right arm in the area that has an overall measurement of 4 ¾" x ¾".

There is an irregular bloodless abrasion of the anterior aspect of the left thigh extending from immediately above the left knee cap…there are abrasions of both feet…the inner aspect of the skin of the thighs next to the labia majora of the vulva shows a "chaffed" bright red surface. There are bloodless abrasions of the right deltoid region that measures 2½" in diameter…The subungual region of all fingers in both hands show considerable amount of bright red hemorrhage. The palmer aspect of the fingers is dry and wrinkled and has a dark red-purple appearance. There is an irregular linear abrasion of the right half of the lower lip that measures 3½" by 2½." Further description of the neck injuries reveal that, tied to the yellow metal chain that forms a ligature around the neck is a brown colored stocking and woven with it are strands of the 15" to 17" long dark brown hair.

Examination of the neck organs reveal considerable amount of hemorrhage on the underlying subcutaneous tissue as well as the strap muscles of the neck with a fracture of the right ala of the thyroid bone and with considerable amount of hemorrhage into the strap muscles surrounding it. The tongue is protruding and is held in situ by the teeth. There is a moderate amount of frothy red fluid that is seen exuding from the nostrils and mouth.

There are ten lacerations of the scalp. *(Author's note: This, of course, was the work of Bundy's crowbar, a severe beating; no doubt. He struck her at least several times about the head. Authorities believe Bundy picked Laura up on one of the darker and more remote areas of highway 89.)*

Examination of the genitalia; the pubic hair is brown and matted. The vaginal orifice is dilated and contains abundant mucoid light tan to white material. The vaginal canal reveals no foreign bodies. The perineum reveals no other areas of laceration or contusion, excoriation, or abrasion of the labia majora or labia minora. The anus is markedly dilated and shows a surrounding hyperemic bright red glistening mucosa with 2" diameter dilated anal ring. The rectum reveals light brown soft fecal material well forted mass about 1 ½" above the anus.

The internal injuries are confined to the cranium. The areas of hemorrhage extend through the full thickness of the cortex and into the white matter of the brain...

Author's note: This report is from the King County Police, and the investigation was headed by lead Detective Robert Keppel

Evidence at Taylor Mountain Crime Scene Relating to Ted Bundy

The Taylor Mountain area, 3.8 miles south of I-90 on Highway 18, was well known to Bundy. John Cowell, Bundy's cousin, used to hike with Ted east of Issaquah. On one occasion, they were driving in John's car on Highway 17 northbound. They drove slowly by the Bonneville power line road and Highway 18 (entrance to the crime scene), noticing the scenery. John's impression was that Ted may know the Highway 18 area very well. They used to drive through the area in 1972 and 1973.

On 3-1-75, a skull was found by forestry students one thousand feet northeast of the intersection of the power line road and Highway 18. Subsequent searches in the same area discovered two more skulls and three lower mandibles. There were four girls identified from the remains.

The lower mandible was the only portion of Lynda Healy found. Her skull was not located, so damage to the skull was unknown.

One skull and the lower mandible of Susan Rancourt were discovered. Damage to the skull consisted of a fracture on the back. The lower jawbone was in three pieces. The medical examiner concluded that the damage to the jawbone was caused by a strong blunt force, not attributed to an animal. Large amounts of blond hair were found near her skull. It was thought the hair to be Rancourt's since the other victims did not have blond hair. Taylor Mountain is about 80 miles from where Rancourt was missing.

Roberta Parks' skull and lower mandible were found. There was no apparent damage to the lower mandible. Her skull was missing the entire upper row of teeth. It appeared Parks sustained a blunt force blow to the upper jaw. There was a third piece of skull that articulated with both the main portion of skull and the lower mandible. There was dark hair found but it is unknown if it belongs to Parks. Taylor Mt. is about 270 miles from Corvallis, Oregon.

The only portion of Brenda Ball found was her skull. Her lower mandible was not located. The right side of Ball's skull sustained a blunt force blow. A portion of the right side skull is missing. It is the opinion of the medical examiner that this was not caused by an animal. Taylor Mountain is about 20 or 30 miles from where Ball was last seen. No clothing or personal belongings of the woman were found.

Bundy left Seattle to attend law school in Salt Lake City in September 1974. The final similar homicide in the northwest occurred August 2, 1974, in Vancouver, Washington. Missing women and female homicides began in the Salt Lake area in October 1974.

Two homicide victims have been found in Utah. Both victims had sustained blows to the head, similar to the damage on skulls found on Taylor Mountain. The Utah victims were also strangled. Both had anal sexual assault. The victims were not found in the same place, but were dropped in remote areas 20-30- miles from the place last seen. A nylon stocking and necklace were found around the neck of each victim. No other clothing or any personal belongings of the victims were located.

One victim was found in Colorado. Blows to the head were received by this victim. Due to decomposition, strangulation is unknown.

Further information relating to Bundy and missing and murdered women in Utah and Colorado appears later.

Author's note: The following report is from the King County Police, and is part of the investigation into the murder of Denise Naslund who was led away from Lake Sammamish State Park and murdered on July 14, 1974. Denise was one of two victims who disappeared from the park that day, as Bundy had earlier led Janice Ott away from the site by way of a ruse. Both women would die together before nightfall.

Summary of facts connecting Bundy to the death of Denise Naslund:

In the Summer of 1974, Naslund was living with her boyfriend, Ken Little. On July 14, 1974, they and another couple drove to Lake Sammamish State Park. Naslund was a business school student.

They arrived at the park about 1:30 p.m. and got a spot on the grass near the spot where the Rainier Band was playing. Denise took 3 or 4 valiums and was feeling high. The weather was hot and there were 40,000 people at the park.

Earlier in the day, Janice Anne Ott left the park with a man dressed in a white t-shirt, white shorts, and white shoes. He had his left arm in a sling. He has been positively identified by two witnesses as Ted Bundy. He had approached Ott saying he needed help loading his sailboat on his car. He had used the same approach with Janice Graham 10 minutes prior to his contact with Ott. Graham also observed Ott and the man leave the park together, walking from the beach towards his brown VW.

Other witnesses at Lake Sammamish were approached by a man similar to the one who left the park with Janice Ott. Prior to the time that Naslund disappeared, other witnesses came into contact with this man.

Sindi Siebenbaum, sixteen years old, was approached by a man with his arm in a sling near the restrooms about 4 p.m. The man said, "Excuse me, young lady, could you help me launch my sailboat?" He said he had sprained his arm and couldn't find anyone to help him. He said the boat was up on the beach and it would only take a few minutes to launch it.

Sindi declined to help him. He seemed to be a little more persistent and pulled on her arm. She described him as blue-eyed, appearing nervous, 6' tall, about 30 years old, and wearing white boxer swim trunks, a long-sleeved pale shirt with stripes.

Jackie Terrell was a forty-seven year old housewife who was at the park with her family. At a little after 1600 she saw a young man near the restrooms. He was wearing his left arm in what looked like a sling, homemade style. Terrell took particular interest because she had just gotten over a broken arm and had a sling. Next to the sling was a yellow ribbon. She did not see him approach any girls.

Patricia Turner, eighteen years old, was walking on the sidewalk, near the concession stand, when she was approached at about 4:15 p.m. The man who approached her had his left arm in a sling and was wearing a white T-shirt, white shorts, and white tennis shoes. He followed her and said, "I need to ask a really big favor of you. I wouldn't normally ask this favor, but my brother is busy and unable to help." He asked for help loading his sailboat. He pointed toward the parking lot with his left elbow. Turner declined to help him and he moved off into the crowd.

Jacqueline Plischke, twenty years old, rode her bike to the park around 4:00 p.m. As she rode along the sidewalk, she noticed a guy watching her. She noticed he had a sling on his left arm. At about 4:20 p.m., the same guy approached her at the far end of the beach near the location of his initial contact with Janice Ott. He said, "I was wondering if you could help me put my sailboat on my car. I'm not very strong." "It's better that I ask someone who was alone."

She declined and said she was waiting for someone. He was very nice about being rejected and wasn't pushy. She has tentatively identified the man as Ted Bundy.

Naslund awoke from a nap around 4:20 or 4:30 p.m. She got up and walked toward the restrooms. That was the last time she was seen by her friends. Betty Berry positively identified her as being in the restroom with another girl, but didn't see her leave with Bundy or any men with slings. Bundy has been positively identified as being at the park prior to Naslund's disappearance. The possibility that he knew Denise is very unlikely as they traveled with a different class of people. Naslund frequented the Flame Tavern as did another victim, Brenda Ball.

There are no witnesses to associate Bundy with Naslund as there was with Ott, but since their remains were found together, it can be assumed that Bundy also had made contact with Naslund as well.

Author's note: What follows is from the King County Police Department file of Brenda Ball, a victim of Ted Bundy who disappeared from the Flame Tavern in Burien, just south of Seattle- or just after leaving it – in the early morning hours of June 1, 1974. The below named witness did not convey her story to investigators until November 20, 1974.

Evidence of questionable nature:

Julie Willits, barmaid at the Flame Tavern who knew Brenda Ball, reported on 11-20-74, that she saw Brenda leave the tavern, at the approximate time of her disappearance, with a guy who had his left arm in a sling. This witness had been deluged with news of the disappearance of Janice Ott and Denise Naslund and the suspect in those cases wore a sling on his left arm.

Information is currently being developed regarding Bundy cashing a check drawn on a White Center bank for three dollars. White Center is just a few blocks from Burien.

Author's note: The following is the transcript of the Intermountain Crime Conference, held in Aspen on November 13 - 14, 1975. While I will be using some of it (highlights, really), much of it will not be repeated here for a couple of reasons. First, some of it is widely known, and has been repeated, not just in my previous two Bundy books, but in this one as well; not to mention all the works from other Bundy biographers. Instead, I will pick and choose the information that stands out in the transcript that is worthy of publishing here. Lastly, there are numerous mistakes in the report. This is natural, due to not only the volume of information presented, but also because some of the information was very new to the detectives. It would be a while before these errors would come to light and be corrected. Those who are extremely familiar with the Bundy case will notice some of these – maybe most of these- but the casual reader will not.

On November 13, 1975, a meeting was held in Aspen, Colorado, for representatives of various police agencies from Washington, California, Utah, and Colorado, to discuss cases of great similarity regarding homicides of young females occurring in these states. The meeting was opened at approximately 9:00 a.m. with a welcoming speech delivered by Carrol D. Whitmire, Sheriff of Pitkin County. A brief welcome was also extended by Lt. Bill Baldridge, of the Pitkin County Sheriff's Department, outlining the purpose of the meeting.

Detective Robert D. Keppel, of the Department of Public Safety, King County Police Department, Seattle, Washington, was introduced. In the summer of '72, he *(Bundy)* took frequent bike trips around Green Lake with Sandy Gwinn, as well as sailing on Lake Washington, and he also went to Lake Sammamish State Park with Sandy Gwinn. He also visited Sandy's parents at their Alpenthal condominium, at which time Karen Covach (Lynda Healy's roommate) met Bundy. The Alpenthal is located at a ski area east of Seattle. At this time, the expenses of these dates were on Sandy Gwinn as Bundy didn't have any money. In July 1972, Edna Cowell (a relative of Bundy's from Arkansas) came up from Arkansas to visit Lynda Healy's roommates, who were friends of hers. It was not established that Bundy knew Healy, but after her disappearance, he would go over to her apartment frequently to visit her roommates.

The previous year, Bundy and his cousin's son were known to go riding and look at old barns. They wouldn't go in the barns, but look at them. Bundy, during this time, would slow down at the area the bodies were later found.

When Bundy was arrested the second time, he had a different apartment with little clothing found. After the first arrest, he was placed on a twenty-four hour surveillance, and during this period he joined the Mormon Church, and with a church group went on an outing near Bear Lake. During this time, investigators also asked to photograph his car and took pictures of his back seat which had a long tear at the top of the back seat which matched the earlier description of a witness. Bundy never asked investigators why his car was being photographed. Bundy bailed out of jail on the possession of burglarious tools charge. The Murray girl positively identified the car. In the meantime, the car had been changed. The hubcaps were different, the car was shinier, possibly having been sprayed with some type of shiny material. The passenger door was a different color and the car had a new front bumper. When Bundy was asked about this, he said he was getting ready to sell the car, which he did two or three weeks later.

Melissa Smith (*Author's note: She was abducted on 10-18-74; more from the record on this abduction and murder later in the book)* was found on 10-27-74 in oak brush in Summit County, nude with a nylon stocking around her neck. She had been beaten around the head and strangled. Drag marks were found on her body, similar to the Campbell victim. Bundy apparently was seen the night of this occurrence soliciting girls to help with his auto. At the time he was first seen, it was noticed he was calm and neat in appearance. He was seen later that same evening in a very disheveled state. The victim (Smith) showed evidence of anal intercourse.

There was a brief talk by Det. Sgt. Butch Carlstadt from Sonoma County Sheriff's Dept. in Santa Rosa, California. He spoke about eight female homicides from February, 1972, through December, 1973. He said that they could not connect Bundy with any of their homicides. Captain Jim Caulfield, also from Sonoma County, then spoke and he brought out the fact that the University of Nevada had offered to computerize all the data on the homicides that had occurred in these states, and see if they could be of some assistance in the solving of these crimes. Captain Caulfield stated that if any agencies were interested, they should contact him and submit any information they had. He mentioned that names could be redacted if so desired.

Mention was then made of another suspect, Daniel A. Aspido, who is currently on death row in New Mexico. His FBI # is 958056D.

Fisher (*Author's note: This is Mike Fisher, the Colorado investigator working on the Caryn Campbell case*) also stated that in March of 1975, a ski instructor in Aspen was approached by a crippled guy to help him with his brief case. She is coming to Aspen to look at the picture of Bundy.

It was noted that Bundy and Harris were both in Aspen at the time of Campbell's abduction. Campbell had to have gone willingly, as there were plenty of people around at that time of night who would have noticed unusual actions. The parking lot of the Wildwood Inn is seventy-five yards away from the Inn. It could be reached from the second story of the Wildwood by a staircase, as the Inn is built on the hillside giving access by several steps to the main level of the street from the second story. This building is such that you can either use the elevator or go down the steps; the rooms each lead to an outside balcony arrangement. Campbell disappeared between 7:40 p.m. and 8:30 p.m. She was officially reported missing at 10:30 p.m.

Investigator David Bustos of Vail Police Department then told of a missing girl from Vail, Colorado. Julie Cunningham, age twenty-six, worked for a sports shop in Vail and did part-time ski instructing. She had worked there two years. On March 15, 1975, she left another apartment in her apartment complex at approximately 6:30 p.m. to return to her own apartment, which she did. She talked to her mother on the phone long distance at 8:30 p.m. She was then supposed to meet her roommate at a bar two blocks from her apartment for a drink between 9:00 and 9:30 p.m. In leaving her place, she would probably walk to the meeting place by taking East Meadow Drive for seven hundred feet across a covered bridge to the mall at Vail. Ore Creek Drive was another road she could have taken from her apartment but it was in the opposite direction of her destination. Investigator Bustos went through her apartment thoroughly. Her apartment was extremely clean, with few clothes as there was little closet space, just casual clothing and clothing for skiing. It was his opinion from talking with her roommate, who knew the victim's clothing well, that she was wearing a brown suede coat, ski hat, jeans, and boots when she left. The subject was a very popular girl. She was well-liked and outgoing, but not a loose girl. The investigator concluded after talking to guys she has dated, that she wasn't easy, but wasn't a prude either. Her diaphragm, which her roommate stated she wouldn't go across the street without, was found in her bedroom drawer, along with her car keys, wallet, toilet articles, favorite coat, special face soap for a skin problem, etc. The victim had just returned from a ski trip with a guy to Sun Valley. She had taken two weeks off, instead of the one week that she had asked for, which was unusual for her inasmuch as she was considered very dependable. It was speculated that the reason for this was that she had found a guy she wanted to settle down with. The trip had not been too good, as when they arrived in Sun Valley, the man she had gone with met some of his former girlfriends. Cunningham was a little depressed about this and had mentioned it to her mother in their conversation of March 15, 1975. Gas was purchased by Bundy in Dillon and Silverthorne, Colorado, on March 15,

1975. Dillon and Silverthorne are close to Vail. Of note, is the fact that these two towns are only 1.3 miles apart. The man who runs the Silverthorne station definitely recognizes Bundy. Also, the Chief of Police of Silverthorne recognized Bundy. The chief had to go to court in Breckenridge, Colorado, and had stopped by the Holiday Inn in Frisco, also near Vail. As he was waiting in the lobby to be seated in the coffee shop,he remembers Bundy coming in, spotting him, then turning and leaving. He was wearing a wet look blue ski jacket and a yellow turtleneck shirt. In Silverthorne, the station remains open until midnight. Bundy only purchased 1.9 gallons, or eighty-nine cents worth, of gas. The Dillon attendant remembered the car but not Bundy. He gassed there in the afternoon.

Author's note: Kathy Parks was abducted (by way of a ruse) from Oregon State University on May 6, 1974, after Bundy made contact with her at the Memorial Union Commons cafeteria around 11:00 p.m. and convinced her to leave with him. What follows is some of the communication the Parks' family had with the chief campus investigator, William R. Harris. It is of interest to note that in one popular Bundy book, Harris is portrayed as believing early on that Kathy's disappearance was the result of foul play. While that may indeed be true, that is not the impression one gets when reading his correspondence of the case. Without question, the investigation into her disappearance was in full swing from the moment Kathy vanished, and Harris did an excellent job pursuing answers into Kathy's disappearance (he was, in fact, doing everything possible to find the answers to her strange disappearance). Yet two months after the abduction, he responded to a Jim Erickson of the Tacoma News Tribune, dated July 19, 1974: "There has been no evidence found to indicate foul play in her disappearance, and her emotional state of mind indicates she might have intentionally left this area, and does not want to be found." Now, it may be Harris expected foul play from the start, but felt required to hold to the "no evidence of foul play" line, as there really wasn't any evidence of it (cops do this all the time). That said, it's apparent that, by July, Kathy's parents were already considering the possibility that their daughter had been murdered. Not only that, but Mr. Parks started to put two plus two together, linking her disappearance to the missing women in Washington State. It was also in July of that year, that Harris, perhaps for the first time, all but admits in a Seattle newspaper article published on July 28th, that foul play is a possibility. What follows is Charles Parks' insightful letter, dated July 17, 1974:

Mr. William R. Harris
Chief Investigator, Campus Security
Oregon State University
Corvallis, Oregon 97331

Dear Bill,

This is to acknowledge and thank you for your most recent report. Nothing has occurred here in any way to give any indication that Kathy might have called. While I know that in your opinion there is little connection between Kathy's disappearance and the four girls in other Washington and Oregon universities in the first five months of the year, I am beginning to think that there might be a connection. Along with other similarities, one more can be added, and that is that none have (sic) been solved.

In any event, I would appreciate any knowledge or information that comes to your attention regarding the other disappearances as well as any involving Kathy, and again, I want to thank you for your dedication.

Yours very truly,
Charles E. Parks, Jr.

Author's note: By September of that year, Harris openly acknowledged the probability of foul play, and soon after this acknowledgment, the remains of Kathy Parks were found, along with those of other victims, at Taylor Mountain in Washington. Taylor Mountain was one of two "dump" sites Bundy used to dispose of his victims.

Finally, it isn't often when one finds a memorial to a crime victim in a homicide case file. Indeed, it's not something that would even enter the mind of any researcher as they're going about their tasks, so when you see one you take notice. The following memorial, written by Kathy's grandfather, Charles Parks, Sr., has been preserved, just like any other piece of evidence in the Roberta Kathleen Parks' file, within the massive King County collection pertaining to the Bundy case, located in the city of Seattle. One can only imagine the pain that was present as Kathy's grandfather penned these words. What follows is from the introduction.

KATHY
A Biographical Memorial
1954 – 1974
By
Charles E. Parks

This is a biographical memorial of my granddaughter Kathy Parks, second daughter of my son, Charles E. Parks, Jr, and his wife, Katherine.

You will find it somewhat different from the customary memorial of this nature. It incorporates the latest chapter of the Parks Family History, which describes in some detail Kathy's abduction, the investigation of her disappearance, the discovery of her remains, and the final acts in the tragedy.

It then gives a brief biography of Kathy, tells of incidents in her life I am familiar with, and then gives an analysis of her character. This character analysis is based largely on an analysis of her relations with her immediate family and others, and on certain letters and notes she wrote reproduced here. After reading these letters, I realized that I did not really know my granddaughter during her lifetime. You, too, will have a better understanding and truer picture of the kind of girl she was and the kind of woman she hoped to be after reading them.

Because of its very personal nature, the text is often presented in the first person and addressed to the reader in the second person. My relationship with Kathy and with many readers makes this possible.

To visualize Kathy as she really was, the portfolio of pictures depicting her at all ages and her brief and tragic life is not included in this memorial. However, the portfolio will be found in the Parks Family History to which all members have access.

Charles E. Parks
October 1975
Orchid Springs
Winter Haven, Florida

The Jerry Thompson Reports

Author's note: What follows are the reports pertaining to

the Bundy murders in Utah. As with the Washington State material (which contained some Utah case files), these reports have not been seen by the general public to any great degree. Utah has never been interested in preserving the Bundy material and housing it in an archive, so finding these today can be more than a little daunting. In fact, the Utah court destroyed the transcript of the DaRonch trial nine years after its conclusion, just as they do with all trial transcripts once they reach that nine year limit. Only a very small portion has made its way into the Washington State and Florida archives, and what they house for Utah can hardly be called a collection. As such, it gives me great pleasure to be able to fully transcribe them here for posterity. I received these reports directly from Jerry Thompson, the retired homicide investigator from the Salt Lake County Sheriff's Office, after he agreed to help me when I was writing The Bundy Murders. Jerry was also lead investigator for the Bundy case in Utah.

Retired Detective Jerry Thompson and his wife when they were in Louisville, Kentucky in May 2005

Criminal Homicide – Melissa Smith

On 8-21-75 this officer made contact with Theodore Robert Bundy, DOB 11-24-46, who lives at 565 First Avenue # 2, phone 531-7286. He was in the county jail at this time, taken out by Sgt. Bernardo and Detective Bob Warner. They met me at the county jail at approximately 6:30 p.m. Previous to this time, a consent search of his home was signed by him and Detective Forbes. We went to the individual's home, which is an upstairs apartment, and searched the home. As we entered the door, there was a pair of skis and a ten-speed bicycle, white in color, brand Peugeot, serial number 1695468. The apartment was very immaculate, in this detective's opinion. The individual had a small room made into an office with a desk and had numerous amounts of law books, several cases on the laws of evidence and criminal proceedings. A thorough search was made of this apartment by myself and Sgt. Bernardo. The only thing of significant value to this detective, which was taken by this officer, was a book called, "The Joy of Sex", a road map of the state of Colorado, a Colorado Ski Country Guide 1974 and 1975, a brochure from the Bountiful Recreation Center, a copy of a Chevron gasoline bill listed to THEODORE ROBERT BUNDY, and also a copy of a phone bill for the month of June, which listed a telephone call to Denver, Colorado. The subject in the case was shown the items and asked if he minded if I took them, and he stated no, there would be no problem. He was very, very cooperative throughout the search and conversation. At no time did he ever ask me what I was searching for, what I wanted to talk to him about, or what was going on. He was asked for his permission if I could take pictures of his Volkswagen car, which was parked out in the back of his apartment. He stated that there would be no problem whatsoever. Pictures were taken of the vehicle by this detective with a Polaroid camera, of the white or light grey in color Volkswagen. In the back seat was a large tear on the top of the seat. It was very evident from the search that the individual had been involved in the political field in the state of Washington. The individual stated that he was in his third year of law at the University of Utah. He stated that he came to Salt Lake in September 1974 to this particular apartment and went to school up here at the University of Utah. He stated that he had moved down here in a truck, an older model one, that wasn't running now, and also had this particular Volkswagen in Washington when he was there. It was registered in the state of Utah in November 1974. Before finding the items from Colorado, he was asked by this officer if he had ever been to the state of Colorado or if he had any friends over there. He stated he had never been there and he didn't know anyone over there. He was asked about the items from Colorado. His immediate response was, "They were left here by a friend of mine who was talking about how good the skiing was over there." He was asked if he had ever been to Bountiful or if he knew where it was at. He stated, "Is that the city just north of Salt Lake? I've heard about it and probably driven through it, but I've never been there to speak of." He was asked about the little brochure from the Recreation Department. He stated, "That was a friend of mine that left it there, some kid of his or something that went up there to some kind of deal."

After thoroughly searching the apartment and taking the above items, I then went out in the back and checked through the car and took some Polaroid pictures of his vehicle. The subject was then returned to the county jail by Sergeant Bernardo. Previous to going there, he was asked if he would mind coming in the next day and talking to Captain Hayward and myself. He stated there would be no problem, he would certainly be there. He never did ask what for or why. The following morning, a phone call was received by Detective Forbes from Defense Attorney John O'Connell stating that he had advised Mr. Bundy not to come into the office and not to talk to us and that he was there for rescinding the consent search warrant that the individual had signed. He was informed that we had already served that search warrant and we didn't need it any more anyway. He stated that he didn't want his client to talk to us. He made the statement, "What are you looking at? You're certainly not looking at him in regards to the murder of all these girls." He was informed no, we just wanted to talk to him. He stated, "I have advised him not to talk to you."

The very next day, Mike Fisher, from the District Attorney's Office in Aspen, Colorado, and Bill Baldridge, from the Sheriff's Office in Aspen, were contacted by this detective and informed about this subject. On their request, a picture of him and a picture of his vehicle, several of them, were mailed over to them. They were informed of the items from Colorado and what we had. They were very much concerned over this individual and wanted to work hand in hand with us on this subject. They are running down at this time the Chevron credit card to see if they can put him in the state of Colorado, and the phone number that was on the phone bill was checked out to belong to the Denver Post Newspaper Agency. Also, a picture of the subject and the vehicle were sent to the Grand Junction Sheriff's Office in Mesa County, Colorado, and the information given to them. All the information, pictures, etc., were also sent to Seattle, Washington, by Detective Forbes and a conversation was made with them over the same subject (see his follow-up). Bountiful Police Department, Lieutenant Ballentine, and Detective Ira Beal were also notified of the situation. They came to our office and received pictures, etc. of the individual. The pictures were taken up to Bountiful and shown to the one female witness who observed the suspicious person on the night of the Debra Kent disappearance. She pulled the picture from a group, stating, "If you put a mustache on this individual, I'm sure that's probably him." The pictures of the Volkswagen and also of the subject were taken and shown to the Murray girl by this detective. In looking at the pictures of the Volkswagen, she stated, "I believe this could be the Volkswagen, but I cannot make a positive identification. The tear looks and resembles the one that I remember seeing." In going through the pictures, she pulled out Mr. Bundy's picture in her hand, gave the pictures back to this officer, stating, "I don't see any one in there that resembles him." She was asked what the one was doing in her hand. She stated, "Oh, here." I asked her if that was the guy or why she pulled it out. She stated, "Oh, I don't know, ah, I guess it looks something like him." She was asked if she was afraid to identify him, and she stated "no." She said, "That looked maybe something like him." She really just didn't know, she didn't think she could identify him if she saw him again or not. This is a very poor witness in this detective's opinion, and I don't know if she can identify the individual or if she is scared or what the situation is. As of this date, communication is still going on with several other agencies by this detective and Detective Forbes. They are attempting to come up with a line-up on this individual through Bountiful and possibly some of the other states' witnesses coming in. It has not been set up as yet.

On 9-3-75 contact was made with Chief Criminal Attorney Bill Hyde and Clint Balmforth from the County Attorney's office. This case was explained to them and a request for a subpoena action against Mountain Bell telephone requesting the information on the subject's telephone from March of 1974 through March of 1975 was made, to which a subpoena was drawn up and will be taken to Judge Leary's chambers to get signed.

Author's note: What follows is a portion of Bundy's arrest record of August 16, 1975, from the Salt Lake County Sheriff's Office   After Bundy was stopped by Sgt. Bob Hayward, Detective Ondrak was called to the scene. This is his report:

At this time, the suspect was arrested by Officer Hayward for evading a police officer. The suspect was informed by reporting officer that the county attorney would be contacted on 8/19/75 and a complaint would attempt to be obtained on possession of burglary tools. On 8/19/75 reporting officer contacted Deputy County Attorney Jack Hiatt of the Kearns Substation and a complaint was issued for possession of burglary tools and a warrant was issued by Judge Bernard for this offense. On 2/21/75 reporting officer contacted the suspect and served the warrant. I booked the suspect in the Salt Lake County Jail. At the time of apprehension, the suspect had in his possession in the back of a brown Volkswagen car, two door, one brown canvas overnight bag. In this bag was one nylon white rope approximately seven feet in length. One tan with dark brown stripe ski mask, one brown cotton glove with a leather hand grip, one Sears model 6577 pry bar, one black leather ski glove, one pair of pantyhose with eye and nose holes cut out, one box of Glad trash bags, one Eveready Captain's brand flashlight, one piece of orange wire, four feet in length, one ice pick with red handle, eight strips of white sheet material cloth different lengths and widths. Also, the suspect had one pair of Jana (made in Spain) handcuffs in the trunk of his car. These items were retained by reporting officer, marked and placed in the Sheriff's evidence room. When the subject was questioned concerning these items, he stated that the items just happened to be junk that he had collected over the year. Reporting officer asked him if it was his junk and at this time he stated, "Yes, it was." Also reporting officer asked him for an explanation for his presence in this area at this hour of the night. The suspect stated that had just been out driving around. There was really no reason for him to be there. The suspect was very cooperative to reporting officer and other officers at the scene. No further additional information.

Author's note: What follows is from the Salt Lake County Sheriff's Office homicide report of Melissa Smith. Melissa was the daughter of Midvale, Utah, police Chief Louis Smith. Chief Smith, completely devastated by the loss of Melissa, asked his friend, Jerry Thompson, to take over the investigation, and Jerry agreed. This report was typed up by Detective Ben Forbes (responding officer to the Melissa Smith crime scene) on 10-29-74. Forbes, no doubt with a great sense of satisfaction, would later have the opportunity to taunt Smith's killer in the not-too-distant future. In this report, the detective mentions that Melissa had a bullet wound in her head- complete with powder burns- but this was not the case, and was an easy mistake to make. The damage was done from the crowbar only, Bundy's weapon of choice that he used on most of his victims.

Address of Occurrence: Approximately 50 yards northeast of eastern boundary of Timberline/Summit County.

Victim: Smith, Melissa

Address: 180 Fern Drive, Midvale, Utah

ELEMENTS OF INVESTIGATION:

Body of a young white female American found on a hillside in the oak brush east of Summit Park Subdivision in conditions which would lead investigating officers to believe that this is an obvious homicide. Mountainside covered in oak brush.

WEAPONS USED: One navy blue sock used for the purpose of strangulation; some type of blunt instrument, possibly a rock.

Discovered by PHILLIP D. HUGHES. Further details on Mr. Hughes are contained in Sheriff Ron Robinson's report. It [the victim's body] was found by Mr. Hughes in the location described in item #3

At approximately 4:00 p.m. on 10-27-74, this reporting officer received a phone call from Sheriff Ron Robinson of Summit County informing me that he had a homicide on his hands and that the nude body of a young white female American had been found on a hillside east of Summit Park Subdivision by some deer hunters. At this time he requested my assistance at the scene. He also informed me that he had attempted to contact Capt. Hayward through the office but had been unsuccessful. I informed Sheriff Robinson that I would respond to the scene and make attempts to contact Capt. Hayward. After I hung up the phone from talking to Sheriff Robinson, I called Capt. Hayward's residence and he had already been informed of the situation, and he himself was en route to the scene. We agreed to meet at the Skyline Café at the Summit Park Subdivision. When we arrived at the Skyline Café in Summit Park, we were met by Sheriff Robinson and some of his deputies and were led into the scene of the actual crime.

The crime scene will be as follows:

The location of the crime scene is approximately due east

of the Summit Park Subdivision, bordering Timberline Subdivision. The actual area of the crime scene itself is mainly predominated by fairly heavy scrub oak and innersparsed (sic) small pine trees. In some fairly tall scrub oak is the body of a white female American, present age unknown, appears to be about 5'4" to 5'5" tall, approx. 110 to 115 pounds. Auburn-reddish hair. Around the neck of the victim is a necklace made of wooden beads, mostly yellow with blue and red beads about every three inches around the necklace. Also around the neck of the victim is what appears to be a man's navy blue knit sock, and this is tied behind the neck of the victim. The body is located on its stomach with the left arm completely folded underneath the body and the right arm extended and unfolded at a 90 degree angle and both legs bent at the knees. There are heavy predominant abrasions over the left and right shoulder blades, and these extended down to almost the small of the back. There are also heavy abrasions on both buttocks and large scrape marks on both buttocks, with more abrasions on the left leg from the knee extending down approximately 8 inches towards the foot. On closer examination of the head of the victim, approximately 6 inches above the top vertebra is what appears to be a bullet wound of contact, approximately one-half inch by one inch, and this is circumferenced by powder burn of approximately one-eighth inch in diameter. There are what appears to be livermortis (sic) marks on the central part of the back, and as far as rigor mortis is concerned, the lower limbs are fairly rigid at this inspection, but the arms and hands are fairly limber. I would estimate the time of death anywhere from 30 to 36 hours.

Author's note: In my first book, I present a theory that I "know" must be true, but there isn't any way to definitively prove it. That said, there is a weight of circumstantial evidence pointing in that direction, and it was validated even further last year when retired Utah investigator, Dennis Couch, released the tapes of Bundy's last confession (made only hours before his execution). Anyway, here's the story; plus, a correction that needs to be addressed.

During 2007 and 2008, when I was doing my original research and working with retired Colorado investigator, Mike Fisher, he told me that he believed Bundy had brought some of his victims to his apartment at 565 First Avenue, a rooming house close to the University of Utah. This includes Debra Kent, as Bundy made a phone call from his apartment to his girlfriend Liz, back home in Washington State, less than thirty minutes after abducting her. I absolutely believe two other victims were there as well: Melissa Smith and Laura Ann Aime; both of whom Bundy kept alive (most likely in a coma from their extensive skull fractures) for a number of days before killing them and disposing of their bodies. Now, Detective Fisher believed that Ted may have kept them in the utility room, but I didn't think so. For one thing, it's too small, and of course, there would be a greater chance of discovery there. No, I believed from the moment we discussed this, that two things occurred: First, because Bundy had no other locations, that we know of, where he could take them (and keep them for extended periods of time), his apartment would be the safest place to temporarily house the victims. And second, he would have absolutely no compunction carrying them up and down the steps late at night (once in and once out), just as he had whisked Lynda Ann Healy away from her rooming house in the busy University District at the University of Washington in the early morning hours of February 1, 1974. Bundy was a bold killer, and it's something he would have done, as he loved taking risks which the average killer did not.

Now, before we leave this subject altogether, it has recently come to my attention that there is also at 565 an underground storage area that was covered with a type of awning that lifts up to reveal steps, where, according to one of the residents, Bundy would go down late at night. This being the case, this is yet a third option as to where he may have kept victims; even perhaps a likely place. However, in my view, he wouldn't have kept Melissa Smith in this underground area, as he had her for at least five days, if not more, and the chance of discovery in this storage area would have been exceedingly high for that extended period of time. It would have been far safer for him to have kept her upstairs and locked away in his apartment. A quick trip up the steps in the middle of the night would have worked for Bundy. For Debra Kent, however, this underground area would probably be exactly where he'd have hidden her, as he only had Kent for one day (according to what he told Utah Detective Dennis Couch) at his apartment before disposing of her body. So, in my view, Bundy likely used his second-floor apartment as well as this storage area for his diabolical activities. Now, moving on to the correction:

In my book, The Bundy Murders, I used a photograph I took of his rooming house at 565 First Avenue, and the view includes his 2nd floor apartment, complete with fire escape in the upper right portion of the photo. The caption of the photo reads as follows: "Bundy's rooming house at 565 First Avenue, near the University of Utah. Bundy maintained an upstairs apartment, and may have carried some of his victims either up the stairs or by way of the fire escape to what one detective believed was his "lair."

Although I believe they were, in fact, ensconced inside this "lair" with Bundy for a time, I say he "may" have carried, etc., because we have no actual proof. There were two openings to his apartment, his door on the second floor as well as the fire escape, so I included them both; although, I see the entrance or exit by way of the fire escape highly unlikely and almost downright impossible IF the configuration of the fire escape was exactly the same in 1974 as it is today. In my view, it just didn't happen. My belief is that he carried them upstairs long after dark when the coast was clear, and there is little difference here than what he did with Lynda Ann Healy back home in Seattle when he carried her out of her basement apartment in the University District.

Now, although I have it right in the caption concerning the two entrances into Bundy's apartment (leaving the reader to think about it), in the text, I accidently left an important portion out of the passage, and it's the mention of the stairs. As such, it looks like I'm advocating the use of the fire escape and I'm not. Even before I wrote the book, as I contemplated Bundy taking his victims there, believing they were upstairs, I always felt the stairs was the way he would have done it. It would have been the easiest and safest way for him to do it, and upon publication, it was annoying to me to discover I had left only the "fire escape" mentioned as the means by which this may have been accomplished.

Lastly, while Mike Fisher and I believe these women were actually held at 565 First Avenue, some do not, including certain retired Utah detectives. However, after the aforementioned tapes were released by Couch, Bundy states on tape that he took Debra Kent up to his apartment! As far as I'm concerned, and no matter where on the property they were housed, this settles the argument entirely.

Continuing with Det. Forbes report...

ID man Rick Sommers is taking black and white and colored photographs of the body and the surrounding crime scene. We are proceeding now approximately 49 paces directly west of where the body was found. There is located a folding patio chair. This also will be photographed by Sommers.

Report concluded by Detective Ben Forbes

Author's note: The following transcript is taken from the taped interview of Liz Kloepfer (or Kendall, her pen name) after detectives Jerry Thompson and Ira Beal flew to Seattle to obtain information on Ted Bundy. I will not be using all of it, choosing instead to publish those sections that contain the most interesting and relative information pertaining to the case.

Q: (Detective Thompson) …or anything like this?

A: Never.

Q: Okay. His habits, would you say if he's out with a group or he's with somebody, is he a loner or is he one to get, you know, gets in, mixes in with the crowd, or, or what would you say?

A: He mixes in, he doesn't have a lot of close friends.

Q: He doesn't have a lot of close friends?

A: No, well, he didn't up here 'cuz we were together most of the time…

Q: But if he was out with a group, he would, he would get along with them or mix in with them for that time? Is he quite athletic?

A: Yes.

Q: Any particular sports?

A: Well, he plays tennis, handball, plays football.

Q: And he plays handball?

A: Yes.

Q: Has he ever played racquetball?

A: Not that I know of.

Q: Since he moved, now he moved from here in September of 1974, right? What contact have you had with him, since that time, just telephone contact?

A: Yeah, we've talked on the phone a lot, and he came back up here right after the last quarter (?). I went down there...

Q: Last Christmas?

A: Yeah. He came up in January, he came up at the end of June.

Q: You were down there in August and December?

A: Um hum.

Q: August of '75 and December of '74?

A: Uh huh.

Q: Has he ever mentioned, since he was down there during that time, what he was doing, telling you with his time what he was doing, just studying, and what was.

A: No.

Q: Did he ever make any comments about any friends he had made?

A: Yeah.

Q: And what he had done in Salt Lake?

A: Yeah, he said something I wanted to talk to you about, he was smoking a lot of dope.

Q: He was smoking pot quite a bit?

A: Yeah, these guys that live across the hall, and he was smoking it.

Q: Has he ever made a comment to you about the missing girls in the Washington area, has he ever talked about this at all? You said that he thought he was being questioned or a suspect in regards to this in Seattle? Has he ever made any comments?

A: Well, since he's been being investigated?

Q: Yeah. Or before.

A: Well before, when he came up here in June he went over to (?) for three days, his old landlady, landlord, and he came back and he said that he's discovered that it's not a good thing to be named Ted in Seattle, and that's all, first we ever talked about it. He had talked about that quite a bit. The only ...

Q: Did he ... go ahead, I'm sorry.

A: The only time he's mentioned it since he's been arrested is that, um, when I told him that I knew he'd been arrested when he called. The reason I knew was because his landlady told me, and he called her to see Kathy had asked the landlady, and she told him he was a suspect, and then he mentioned at that time, and we didn't talk about it, speechless, and then he had a friend of his who works, well, she writes crime stories, she contacted Kathy to find out what was going on, and he mentioned that it was routine, but Ann (?) had told me that it was a routine investigation.

Q: Do you know who this friend is that writes these crime stories?

A: Yeah, her name's Ann Rule.

Q: It's what?

A: Ann Rule.

Q: Rule?

A: Um hum.

Q: Do you know, is she from Salt Lake?

A: No, she's from here. They had worked together at the Crisis Center up here.

Q: What is she, a writer for just her own or a paper or just works for somebody?

A: No, she writes for just crime magazines. Yeah, she's written a whole book on the missing girls.

Q: That she has written a book on this, you don't know if she has, or you don't know what the book is or anything?

A: No.

Q: Is she a pretty good friend of his?

A: No.

Q: He doesn't have the book, do you know? Has he ever

said he has it or has seen the book?

A: No.

Q: Has he ever made any kind of comments about what the police have in regards to these investigations, that they don't have anything, or anything at all about how they, any details on where any of them have been killed and how they've been killed or anything like this?

A: No.

Q: Has he ever said anything about his Volkswagen, have you ever known it to be any other color than what it is?

A: No.

Author's note: The next set of questions I've omitted as they are of little revelatory importance. Then Liz asked Thompson about a person who came to be known as the "First Avenue Rapist." She was apparently concerned as Ted lived at 565 First Avenue.

Q: Okay. What did you want to ask me?

A: Okay. Oh, this is the most important thing, my father used to, um, in June, before he came up here, he told me in great detail about … that he'd heard on the news, just one time only, about some rapes on First Avenue, which he lives on, and he says they were all college girls, and uh, he said something like the guy had a beard, so that lets me out. And he says that he thought he had an idea who might have done it … retarded people around the corner from him, and one of the guys that was a (?), he had heard on the news.

Q: He called you and told you about this?

A: Yes.

Q: In June of this year?

A: Yes. So he told me that, I can't remember, if he came up or asked me to come up, he says that he called a detective down there, a woman, who was handling the case, and she contacted him about this possible suspect. In June, he started growing a beard and when he was up here he said that this guy he thought was a possible suspect had shaved his head, and he said, "Doesn't that seem really odd to you that he would do that right after the news out?" and I wanted to say no…beard.

Q: And he was growing a beard in June?

A: Um hmm..

Q: Of this year, rather.

A: Um hmm … suspicious of this case of rapes?

Q: Now that would have been handled by the Salt Lake City Police, and they did have some rapes in the Avenues last summer, or this summer, I don't know the month and I don't have any details in regards to the suspect, whether he had a beard, I'll have to check that out. There is a woman detective down there that works rapes. Her name is Pat, and that I don't know, and yes, they did have what they called an "Avenue Rapist."

A: Oh.

Q: What else did you want to ask me?

A: Oh, um, he asked me yesterday if I thought there was (sic) two separate (?), and I do, like, I couldn't put my finger on it until I was talking to Mary Ann *(Author's note: this would be Mary Ann Chino)* about it, but like he was insanely jealous of me.

Q: Very jealous?

A: Yeah, and it, like um, he went so far as to follow me when I went out sometimes, you know, and I thought, I thought that was odd, and the other thing is that he used to take naps in the day, and so therefore he was wide awake at night and he used to go out walking around a lot late at night. A couple of times when I was walking home from meetings he snuck up on me and scared the hell out of me. He was out a lot late at night and it bothered me.

Q: Were the girls up here in the Seattle area publicized to the point that publicity gave the dates when they turned up missing?

A: Um hum.

Q: Okay, and you being familiar with the dates, you told me the other day that those particular dates, the ones you could remember, he wasn't with you. Do you remember anything about those particular dates, the next day, if he got a hold of you, his comments, any way he acted unusual, or did he make any comment about it?

A: No. I'm really ... I ... the only dates I know anything about is the July 14th one, because by that time I was just a little bit suspicious, and I reconstructed what had happened, but I ... I can't find anything, and I've really looked hard, you know, to give me any memories about the other dates.

Q: July 14th when you remember well.

A: Yeah.

Q: What can you tell me about him on that date?

A: He came over in the morning and I was just getting ready to go to church.

Q: That was Sunday?

A: Yes, and it was a sunny day. We had an argument the night before because I wanted to do something and he didn't, um, well, anyway so he came over early in the morning and I said well, I'm going to church and then I'm gonna go lay out in the sun. So he asked me where I was going, I thought maybe he'd meet me there, but he didn't, and I didn't … We quarreled again that morning, and I was really mad at him, so I was really surprised when I got home and he called me about six and said let's go eat, and I was surprised at this. I thought he was mad at me; and so we went out and ate that night.

Q: At six o'clock?

A: Yeah.

Q: Was there anything unusual about him that night?

A: Well, he looked really wiped out, he was getting a bad cold, which really turned into a whopper, but I asked him what he had done and he said he'd laid around and rested, but he looked just so tired, and uh, he told me his (?) were gone.

Q: Okay, let me ask you another personal question, (Redacted, but Liz).In regards to his sex life, was he a type of individual that, from sex, that he could go one right after the other continue, or was he an individual that wasn't, what I'm trying to say, unusual, for the fact that a man if he had intercourse with a girl that he could have one right after the other, or would he be more or less the normal type, did he have an extra strong situation in that line?

A: It's hard to tell, when we first met each other, I mean.

Q: Right, no, I realize that.

A: Yeah right, well after 6 years, you know, he was normal.

Q: Okay. Maybe I shouldn't do this, I hope I got your confidence enough, that you, like I told you yesterday, that you won't talk to him, and perhaps that we can get the doubt out of your mind and maybe a doubt out of ours both, one way or the other. Maybe this will help you. I have a picture here of all the items that we took from his car, and one particular item here you don't know about, and I wanted to ask you something about it. But I will let you look at them first.

A: What's all this stuff?

Q: Okay, now I can tell you. This stuff here is bits of sheets torn in about one or two inch strips, and there are some, that's what basically all that stuff is, and then this is, there is cord and rope in small sections. It's the handcuffs and it's the punch, the gloves, the ski mask, this is a pair of women's pantyhose with eye holes and a mouth cut out. This is, like a canvas gym bag they were all in. This is a bag of those garbage can liner bags, 30 gallon garbage can liners. This is a flashlight and that's the crowbar. Have you ever seen that crowbar before?

A: No.

Q: Have you ever seen any of that stuff before?

A: Yes, I've seen the gloves and I've seen the gym bag.

Q: Have you ever seen what's in the gym bag?

A: No, it was usually empty, he has another one that he carries his, you know, athletics stuff in.

Q: Okay, now this might enlighten you to why we suspect something wrong, very highly unusual, would you say, that any man would have these things, other than for what reason, an armed robbery, maybe? Very much, armed robberies are handled daily with these and these. Of course, we didn't come up with any gun or anything else. And the handcuffs, the rope bindings, what would you surmise they might be in a person's possession for? To tie somebody up, I would assume. So, I can't answer that, but those are the things that was (sic) in his car, and those are the things he was arrested for, and the statute we use is what we call burglarious tools, at 3:00 in the morning, on the west side of Salt Lake, and his explanation was, "I was just driving around, couldn't sleep." I cannot tell you what he was doing. I have no idea. But that's basically one of my concerns. I don't buy his explanation for them. Like I say, even the nylon pantyhose he had an explanation, that he put them on to keep his ears and his face warm when he was skiing, and I says you don't ski in August. "But I just still had them in my car." So I, that's my concern.

A: What about the ice pick?

Q: I can't answer that either.

A: What'd he say?

Q: It was just a house tool, just a thing that he had in his car. But I can't answer that either, I don't know why or what the, but you have never seen the ice pick or any of these other items?

A: Huh uh. I told Kathy, and I double-checked, when he used to drive my car, I noticed that the crowbar, I mean the jack hammer, was taped with adhesive tape, and it still is to this day.

Q: Okay, we'd like to look at it before we leave, some way or another.

Author's note: We skip a few statements that have no real information, and then Liz once again tells of strange things Ted has done:

A: He used to sleep in front of my house (*Author's note: In his car*). He left my house late at night and then he came back and I opened the door to see what he was doing and he came back to get that, and he looked really sick, you know, like he was hiding something, and I says (sic) what have you got in your pocket, and he wouldn't show me, and I reached in and grabbed it and it was a pair of surgical gloves. Weird.

Q: He had them in his pocket? What did he say he was going to do with them?

A: I think he turned around and left. I can't...

Q: And this was in the middle of night?

A: Yeah, it was late at night. It seems incredible as I say all of this that I didn't, you know, say you're weird, go away.

Q: Well no, I realize these things, you know, of course a lot of things you don't have explanation for, you know, and you don't think and with someone else you think, what the hell, you know, something, you don't think of them until later, and that's why, like I say, as things come up just like myself, I think of things different (sic), and you probably will too, and I hope I can still communicate with you. Like I say, if you think of anything, or you want to ask me any questions, and you think of anything else that may be of interest, if you'll call me, and call me collect, you … now you have that card.

Ted Bundy, flanked by two officers, on his way to a Utah court, 1976. Courtesy the Salt Lake Tribune

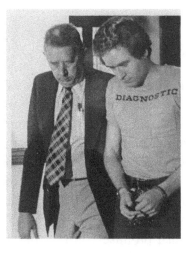

Bundy waits with an officer during a court appearance, 1976 Courtesy the Salt Lake Tribune.

Author's note: Towards the end of the Q&A, Liz asks about Carol DaRonch and her escape from her abductor, an abductor she believes (but doesn't really want to believe) could be her Ted Bundy.

A: I read in the paper long time ago that there was a girl in Salt Lake that had gotten away, that she'd been abducted and the guy tried to handcuff her to him, and I wondered if you had shown his picture to her.

Q: Yes.

A: And?

Q: You put me on a spot, don't you? I can't tell you (redacted, but Liz).

A: Oh God.

Q: I know what you're going to say.

A: The next thing you ask me...

Q: You're going to tell me, "I can't tell you, Jerry, I can't tell you." I'll tell you this much, I will let you know, but I can't tell you right now. I will communicate with you and let you know at a later date, but I cannot tell you, and not only can I not tell you, I can't tell anyone, even fellow officers other than my partner on the case, just what all we're doing and what we have, because we can't take a chance in such a case, any kind of a leak or anything else or losing a piece of evidence publicity wise or anything else, so that's, not that I don't want to tell you, and not that I don't want to do this or that, but I promise you I ... like I say, I hope to keep communicating with you and I will let you know, but I cannot tell you right now. Has he ever mentioned anything about that individual to you?

A: Huh uh.

An incarcerated Ted Bundy, circa 1976. Courtesy Salt Lake Tribune

The Idaho Reports

Author's note: Bundy murdered at least two individuals in Idaho, that we know of. The first was an unidentified hitchhiker he murdered on his way to Utah to attend law school on September 2, 1974. His second was 12-year-old Lynette Culver. He had gone to Pocatello to hunt college women at the university after arriving in the city on May 5, 1975. It was May, and the city was still quite cold and experiencing snow showers on both of the days Bundy was there, which turned out to be a very real hindrance to abduction as he was unable to convince women to go with him. He came upon the kids of Alameda Middle School as they came flooding out of the building at lunchtime. Spotting pretty Lynette Culver, Bundy motioned her over to his car, and invited her inside. No doubt feeling flattered that a grown man would show interest in her, she went with him back to his room at the Holiday Inn, where Bundy drowned the young girl in the bathtub. Then, true to form for this killer, he had sex with her dead body.

I cover this murder fully in <u>The Bundy Murders: A Comprehensive History</u> (where I uncovered new, significant, and never-before published information on the case), as well as some additional aspects of the case in my second Bundy book, <u>The Trail of Ted Bundy: Digging Up the Untold Stories</u>, where, with the assistance of retired Idaho Attorney General Investigator Russ Reneau, I dispel a myth that has surrounded the abduction of Lynette Culver for many years; i.e. that Lynette purportedly wasn't abducted at Alameda Middle School, but had instead walked to another school blocks away and fell victim to Bundy. This was a myth, but one that had never been fully addressed until the publication of my second book on Ted Bundy.

The following report was written by Chief Investigator of the Idaho Attorney General's Office, Russell Reneau.

Compendium of Lynette Culver Homicide Investigation

On May 6, 1975, Lynette Culver, age twelve, was reported missing after she failed to return to Alameda Junior High School in Pocatello, Idaho, following the noon break. The Pocatello Police Department conducted the initial investigation, which failed to develop any useful leads or identify any suspects. While foul play was suspected, Lynette Culver's body had not been found. Sometime later, Pocatello detectives became aware of Ted Bundy, who was at that time in custody in Utah. They had no evidence to connect Bundy to the disappearance of Lynette Culver, but in the absence of any useful leads, decided to attempt to interview him anyway. That effort was thwarted, when Bundy informed Utah authorities that he was unwilling to submit to interviews by any law enforcement officers.

There were no other developments in the Lynette Culver investigation until January 18, 1989, when I was contacted by the Chief Investigator of the Washington Attorney General's Office. This contact led to subsequent conversations with Diana Weiner, an attorney purportedly representing Mr. Bundy in civil matters. As a result of these conversations, an interview of Ted Bundy was scheduled for Sunday, January 22, 1989, at 11:00 a.m., to take place at the Florida State Prison.

Prior to traveling to Florida for the Bundy interview, statewide inquiries were sent to all Idaho Law Enforcement agencies requesting information on unsolved murders and missing person reports on young women. The Lynette Culver case was among several other responses we received which seemed to fit Bundy's crime profile.

During the interview of Ted Bundy, he confessed to committing two murders in Idaho. One of the victims was a hitchhiker who was killed in the fall of 1974. Bundy was unable or unwilling to provide much detail regarding this victim and efforts at locating the body or identifying a matching missing person report have been unsuccessful to date.

The second murder occurred in the spring of 1975, and Bundy provided significant detail about the victim and the manner in which the crime was committed. According to Bundy's account, this victim was abducted near a junior high school in Pocatello, Idaho, and taken to a Holiday Inn where Bundy was staying. He admitted to luring the victim into his vehicle but would not explain the ruse he used. Bundy's recollection of the conversation he had with the victim was quite detailed and included statements from the victim concerning her personal life. These statements included her living circumstances, the fact that her family was planning on moving to a new residence, that she had relatives in the Seattle area, and that she was having a truancy problem at school. Additional information obtained from Bundy indicated that the murder occurred at the Holiday Inn and that the body was placed in a river north of Pocatello. Bundy's description of this location was vague and has not led to the recovery of the remains. Bundy also provided a physical description which matched that of Lynette Culver.

Upon returning to Idaho, the parents of Lynette Culver were contacted and interviewed regarding the statements attributed to the victim by Bundy. We determined that these statements accurately described Lynette Culver's personal circumstances with the exception of the truancy problem. Alameda Junior High School records did reflect, however, that Lynette had numerous absences which had not been reported to her parents. We then reviewed all of the media coverage generated by Lynette Culver's disappearance in 1975 and were able to eliminate the possibility that Bundy could have learned these personal details from those reports.

After reviewing the totality of the information available, we concluded that Theodore Bundy did, in fact, abduct and murder Lynette Culver.

Author's note: Portions of the following report are repeats of previous reports in this same section, but I'm leaving it "in" as it's a part of the official record.

Interrogation of Ted Bundy: Preface

On January 18, 1989, I was contacted by Bob Keppel, Chief Investigator for the Washington Attorney General's office, and informed that Ted Bundy was possibly was going to provide information regarding murders committed in Idaho. On January 19 & 20, 1989, I had several telephone conversations with Diana Weiner, an attorney purportedly representing Mr. Bundy in civil matters. As a result of these conversations, an interview with Ted Bundy was scheduled for Sunday, January 22, 1989, at 11:00 a.m. to take place at the Florida State Prison.

During discussions between the Idaho Attorney General and the Director of the Idaho Department of Law Enforcement regarding a proposed interview, it was decided that two other officers would accompany me to Florida, specifically, Randall Everitt, a criminal investigator with the Idaho Attorney General's Office, and Jim Whitehead, Chief of the Idaho Bureau of Investigation.

At approximately 10:00 a.m. on January 22, 1989, we arrived at the Florida State Prison and met with Paul Decker and L.E. Turner, both of whom are assistant superintendents for the prison. We were provided with prison records and given verbal background information concerning Mr. Bundy. At approximately 11:00 a.m., we met with Diana Weiner and Special Agent William Hagmaier of the FBI, and were advised there would be a delay in the scheduling of the interview. We were also informed that this would be a noncontact interview and that it would be necessary to place tape recorders on both sides of the glass partition.

Prior to the interview, we met with Diana Weiner and Ted Bundy and had an unrecorded conversation regarding preconditions. Diana Weiner asked us to agree on two specific conditions as follows:

1. That we would forward a written document of some type to the Governor of Florida advising him that Mr. Bundy had been cooperative in providing information relating to Idaho murders. Further, that it was our understanding that Mr. Bundy was also attempting to assist other law enforcement agencies in clearing murders in the severe time restrictions allowed. While she did not specifically ask for us to recommend a postponement in Mr. Bundy's execution, there was a clear inference to that effect.

2. That we would hold a press conference immediately following the interview with Mr. Bundy and make the same statements outlined in paragraph #1 above. We agreed in part to the conditions in paragraph #1 and declined to comply with those in paragraph #2.

The interview commenced at 12:02 p.m. The pre-agreed format is that I would ask the questions and that Jim Whitehead and Randy Everitt would pass notes to me with any questions they wished to have posed. Also present during the interview were Diana Weiner and Special Agent Hagmaier. The interview was terminated after exactly one hour.

Since tape recorders had been placed on both sides of the glass, it was necessary to separately transcribe the question tape and the answer tapes and then integrate the two sides of the conversation. During this process we discovered that a portion of the interview recorded on Mr. Bundy's side of the glass had been lost on a self-reversing tape recorder. Since a backup recorder was also used on that side of the glass, we were eventually able to document the entire interview. A copy of that transcript is attached hereto.

Author's note: What follows is the full and complete transcript of the end-of-life interview Ted Bundy gave to the Idaho investigators to clear the two murders he committed in the state. I have used only small portions of this transcript in my first two books on the case, but I will use the entire document for this book. Not only is this a book pertaining to "The Record," but it will be readily available now to researchers in the coming years. Indeed, I was told by one source that the manuscript had disappeared from the Idaho Attorney General's Office. As such, it will be of the utmost importance for future researchers to have access to it.

A correction: in The Bundy Murders, I accidently state that the hitchhiker's destination may have been Wyoming, when in fact I should have written Montana. Nevertheless, I'm glad to make the correction here.

Editing: Within this document there are instances where the word "we're" is spelled "were" while along with this, the proper usage of the word "were" is used as well. In these instances, I have made the proper corrections, for to not do so would create confusion to the readers. There are also a number of places where Bundy responds to the investigator with a "yeah," but it was misspelled by the transcriber as "ya." I have not corrected these, so for clarity's sake, a word to the wise.

Interrogation of Ted Bundy

BUNDY: All right, let's begin with … try to focus in on the

date here ... the period. I believe it's April 1975, possibly May. It's in one of those two months. I traveled from Salt Lake City to, now here is my confusion, to either Pocatello or Idaho Falls, and I tend to think it was Pocatello but I'm not absolutely sure. Trying to recall perhaps the day of the week. Again, I know it was during the week, not on a weekend. I stayed in a Holiday Inn, in, well, in all likelihood, Pocatello, for at least one night. I'm cutting down on a lot of factual stuff right now, you're free to ask. Just to give you the picture. I abducted a young girl from a junior high school, probably in Pocatello.

It's hard to tell from this map. Perhaps if we had a more detailed map of the general vicinity, region of around Pocatello, I might be able to tell you more specifically. But eventually that same day I ... It's a little bit hard, excuse me, to talk about. Get a little bit closer here so my voice won't carry quite so far down the way where the officers are sitting. Later that same day, her body was placed in the river. I don't know what river, again, if I could see a road map, I would be able to better tell you. Probably the Snake River, but, again, I'm not absolutely certain. Again, it's ... I don't know what representations were made to you or what inferences about my activities in Idaho. That's why I felt that I didn't know, if you wanted to be coming down here, all three of you, for me to tell you essentially what I have to tell you. I mean, I'm not telling you about some large number of incidents, crimes, but that's the first incident and if you want to probe into that further to get more information ...

RENEAU: I have just a few questions I would like to ask now. When you ... after the abduction, did you leave the city of Pocatello, and if so, which direction were you headed with her?

BUNDY: I believe it was north.

RENEAU: Okay, do you recall approximately how far out of the city it would have been where her body was placed in the river?

BUNDY: A few miles, it's hard to say … five miles. I mean that would be just a rough guess.

RENEAU: Can you describe the girl for us?

BUNDY: She was in her early teens, long brown hair, was wearing blue jeans, is about all I can remember for sure.

RENEAU: About how tall do you think she was?

BUNDY: 5'2"

RENEAU: Did you ever learn her name during your contact with her?

BUNDY: I may have but I can't recall. I don't recall specifically. I can … there may be a couple of corroborative details that I can give you that might help but, by way of identity they just happened to stick in my mind for reasons that I can't quite, you know, explain really. She made a comment that sounded that she had other friends or relatives in Seattle. The reason I remembered that is, 'cause I've been in Seattle. Made a comment indicating that either she lived with her grandmother or that her grandmother lived with her family. Another comment indicating that perhaps they were thinking of moving to another house, the family was thinking of moving to another house. Indications that she had had some trouble with truancies at school, about missing school and also finally that I encountered her at a time when she was leaving the school grounds to meet someone at lunch time. Those are the … some of the specific kinds of recollections that come to mind immediately. As I say, I don't recall the name of the young lady.

RENEAU: When you stayed at the motel there, did you register under your name or what name, what was it?

BUNDY: I registered under an assumed name, but yes, I didn't register under my name and I could describe the place well. I mean the Holiday Inn, such as it is, but nevertheless, no, I did not register under my own name.

RENEAU: You recall what name you used?

BUNDY: No, in all likelihood it would be a name I would pick out of thin air. I mean, it wouldn't be a name I would remember.

RENEAU: Were you driving? How were you traveling at that time?

BUNDY: I was driving, yes.

RENEAU: What kind of vehicle were you driving?

BUNDY: A Volkswagen sedan, beige.

RENEAU: Where was that vehicle registered?

BUNDY: Utah.

RENEAU: To you?

BUNDY: To me.

RENEAU: Would you have used that license number when you registered?

BUNDY: That's a good question … uh … 'cause you know they often do. Conceivably, you know, 'cause often times I wasn't quite as careful as I should have been, but you know if I … it's possible, but not necessarily likely.

RENEAU: Did you have any encounters, at all, with any law enforcement people during this trip, traffic citations, anything like that?

BUNDY: No, but … no, I may have come close a couple of times, as a matter of fact, but nothing that ended up with an actual contact. There was a contact, but I don't know if you can follow it up. The evening before, it was a campus, a college campus in town and which is the reason it makes me think it was probably Pocatello. Anyway … and I was asked to leave one of the buildings by someone, one of the supervisors, but I don't know if that's an incident that could be recorded anyway.

RENEAU: Remember which building it was you were asked to leave?

BUNDY: If I had … and I can visualize, at least what I think I am visualizing, the campus. By the map I mean, the diagram, it might be able to help me a little bit. I think it's … it was a dormitory, it was a high-rise and it was sort of on the edge of the campus.

RENEAU: Why was it you were asked to leave?

BUNDY: Well, I was just an unauthorized person in the building and couldn't produce any identification so it was on one of the upper floors.

RENEAU: Did you purchase gasoline for your vehicle in Pocatello? And if so, would you have used a credit card?

BUNDY: You know, I wouldn't have for this reason. I can recall this fairly clearly, is because a full tank of gas from Salt

Lake City I was able to make round trip without stopping for gas. That's my recollection. I don't... I seem to feel like I avoided using the credit card in that area at that time.

RENEAU: Did you have any significant contact with anyone else in the Pocatello area during your stay there?

BUNDY: I'm thinking it was a course of two days actually that I was there. No.

RENEAU: What we would like to do Mr. Bundy, if it's all right with you, is move ahead to the other incident you were going to tell us about, then we may come back to this one, if we come up with some other questions. Would that be all right?

BUNDY: Sure, sure, let me ask you this for what it's worth, and I don't want you to betray any specifics or anything, but were you aware of anything like this, any of you, happening during that period of time? If you don't mind, or is that too much...

RENEAU: There were some missing person reports during that period of time. We're going to have to check the details you've given us to see if it fits any of those.

BUNDY: All right. I was just hoping that maybe you were already aware in some way that you would be able to focus in on that. I should probably add that it was a junior high school.

RENEAU: Can you tell me approximately where in town the junior high school was?

BUNDY: Well, in relationship to ... best as I can recall, in relationship to the Holiday Inn it was, sort of like, across town maybe two miles, three miles. You would leave the

Holiday Inn and turn, let's say, left, and I don't know if you would stay on the exact same street but, turn left and move in the direction that would be taking you away from the Holiday Inn after you turn left, and maybe 20 to 30 blocks up a way was the... was the... was the school. (*Author's note: Bundy most likely turned right, and as can be seen with a lot of his geographic testimony for this confession, he isn't sure about a lot of things pertaining to cities, locations, rivers, or roads. Turning right would have put him on Pocatello Creek Road and this runs right into East Alameda, which becomes West Alameda, and Lynette's school is on this road. The distance between the Holiday Inn and Alameda Middle School is about two miles. If Bundy did, in fact, turn left from The Holiday Inn, then he would have had to meander his way at some point onto the correct road.*)

RENEAU: Did this route take you through the center of town?

BUNDY: Well, it's across, well, let's see ... that's a good question. It wouldn't have taken you ... well, I don't think it would have taken you through the center, it wouldn't have taken you through the center of the city. That would be my rough guess, 'cause the center of the city, as I recall, is somewhere south of the school.

RENEAU: Okay, so would you have been traveling principally east or west from the Holiday Inn?

BUNDY: I believe it would've been ... I know it would've been in the northern part of ...

RENEAU: Was there anyone else around at the time that you abducted this girl that might've seen that happen?

BUNDY: Well, there were a number of people there, but

no one seemed to know, that I detected, took any notice, or acted a way that indicated that they were taking notice.

RENEAU: Were you able to get her to go with you voluntarily?

BUNDY: Yes.

RENEAU: Okay, if we could move on to the second one?

BUNDY: In approximately early September, 1974, I was driving from Seattle to Salt Lake City. I was moving. I was passing through Idaho on the highway, maybe it was 84, the freeway. Somewhere just on the outside, very close to, or on the outskirts of Boise, I picked up a hitchhiker traveling. Well, I was traveling east at the time. I'm trying to recall. She was standing down … it wasn't a downtown off-ramp, I mean, on-ramp, but it was further out of the city. Ranch style suburban houses were in view of the off-ramp, on-ramp. It was early evening as I recall. Anyway, I pulled over… My car was full of stuff… She was carrying a large green backpack. I believe she was 16 to 18, light brown hair. About 5'6". My recollection is we stopped… Well, I had no place specific in mind, because it was after dark. It was at that point of the freeway when you first come into any contact with the river. We were driving, somewhere we could pull off the side of the road and drive to the river, get off close to the river. The river would have been on the right hand side of the highway going west.

RENEAU: Excuse me, you said west, but did…

BUNDY: No, that's not right.

RENEAU: Okay.

BUNDY: That's all that comes off the top of my head.

RENEAU: Was her body placed in the river?

BUNDY: Yes.

RENEAU: Do you recall what the area was like to the extent that you could tell in the dark, whether or not it was difficult to get to the water, those kinds of things?

BUNDY: I'm trying to recall. It seems that we didn't have to pull off the freeway, or we could pull right off as opposed to a regular freeway where you had to find an exit. It was a partially paved, partially dirt road that led down underneath a … it may have been a railroad trestle. It was alongside a little creek. The area was sandy as it led out to the riverbank.

RENEAU: When you put this body in the river, was, how was the body attired? Was there clothing or not?

BUNDY: No.

RENEAU: Were there any weights or anything like that attached to the body?

BUNDY: No.

RENEAU: So, can you recall approximately how much time you were with this girl as you were traveling east?

BUNDY: Three hours … four.

RENEAU: Three or four hours, okay. Did she tell you where her ultimate destination was?

BUNDY: My recollection is it was somewhere in Montana.

RENEAU: Did you have the impression she was a runaway or that she was just traveling on her own?

BUNDY: I got the impression that she was leaving home.

Probably from the Boise area.

RENEAU: When you were down by the river, or perhaps some other location, what happened with the clothing and the backpack you described?

BUNDY: The clothing was also put in the river. The backpack went to Salt Lake and it was disposed of along a roadside near a dump.

RENEAU: Did you go through any of the contents before discarding the backpack?

BUNDY: Yes.

RENEAU: Was there anything in there that told you what her identity was?

BUNDY: There was identification in there. It was ... the identification itself was burned.

RENEAU: When you were on this particular trip, which vehicle were you driving at the time?

BUNDY: The Volkswagen.

RENEAU: Same vehicle we discussed before? Was it at that time also registered in Utah?

BUNDY: No, it was registered in Washington.

RENEAU: Again, this would have been approximately September of ... early September '74.

BUNDY: Yes. You could get the exact date because I was purchasing gas along the way with a credit card.

RENEAU: Which kind of credit card was it?

BUNDY: Standard Oil.

RENEAU: Do you recall which places you might have stopped for gas, or which towns?

BUNDY: I made a number of trips back and forth. This particular trip I don't remember, in terms of where I got gas, although Boise was a frequent stop where I got gas.

RENEAU: What name was the credit card in?

BUNDY: Mine. Theodore Bundy.

RENEAU: Can you tell me, if we're to locate this young person's body, what would the physical evidence show us was the cause of death?

BUNDY: Well, I … which are you talking about?

RENEAU: Well, I'm talking about … no, I'm talking about the second one right now.

BUNDY: The one I talked about first? Oh, okay. Well you know, at that point and time, I don't know that you could tell that in a way because so much time has passed, but the cause would have been strangulation.

RENEAU: Would there have been any structural damage?

BUNDY: Possibly, from a blow to the head.

RENEAU: The strangulation … was a ligature of any kind used, and can you tell me which part of the head would have been damaged?

BUNDY: Uh, the right side or right rear.

RENEAU: What type of ligature was used?

BUNDY: A white nylon clothes line cord.

RENEAU: What did you do with the ligature afterwards?

BUNDY: It was left in the … well, wait a minute, let me see. I think it was among the articles of clothing that was (sic) thrown in the river at that time.

RENEAU: Now if we could go back to the first incident for just a moment. Same question, what was the cause of death in that situation?

BUNDY: Uh, it would have been drowning.

RENEAU: And again, would there be any structural damage?

BUNDY: No.

RENEAU: Again speaking about the first incident, which you described, did this girl have schoolbooks or school articles with her?

BUNDY: No. My understanding was, my recollection is that, at the time, she was leaving the school grounds to go meet someone and I assume that she left everything at the school.

RENEAU: Again speaking to the first incident, the junior high school girl, at the time that her body was placed in the river, was she clothed or not?

BUNDY: Yes.

RENEAU: And the clothing … you've already described as blue jeans and what else?

BUNDY: Well, I can't clearly recall now. I'm … I'd be kidding myself if I thought I could. I need to focus in on that a little bit better. Let's see, a jacket of some kind, but nothing really loud color, it wasn't a bright color of jacket that I recall. A pullover top, blue jeans, and shoes, not boots, shoes of some kind.

RENEAU: But not a dress?

BUNDY: No.

RENEAU: You described some things about her circumstances at the time. Is there anything else you can recall about where she was going to meet someone or who that person might have been?

BUNDY: Uh, I recall her saying something that she was going to meet a boy at a nearby park or recreation area center … that's, yes, that's what she seems to have said, what I recall her saying.

RENEAU: Did you get the impression that she was just going there for lunch?

BUNDY: Basically, yes.

RENEAU: If we could go back to the second one just for a minute?

BUNDY: Yes.

RENEAU: Mr. Bundy, when you … after you picked this girl up, you said that you drove near the river, near the freeway. Did you get off on a two-lane road or was it, did you take an off-ramp to get to the river from the freeway?

BUNDY: This is a little after dark by this time. You see, let me try to explain what I remember, the best of what I can recall. As you may remember, back in the 70's … am I recalling this right? I'm trying to remember this now. But portions of this highway that ran close to the river would go back and forth from old construction to new, you know, old construction. I mean the old style highway. And it seems to be shortly after I first noticed the river. It was a clear night, so the river was, well, visible in the same sense that it's visible at night. But no, I don't think I had to take an off-ramp to get to it. I may have been able to get on a side road but it wasn't

… it was like a turn off, and there were some railroad tracks between the highway and the river. I mean a railroad trestle.

RENEAU: And there was a little stream?

BUNDY: What amounted to a little stream that ran down underneath the trestle, which may have been why the trestle was there.

RENEAU: I'm returning to the first incident. Do you recall why you were in Pocatello at that particular time?

BUNDY: Yes.

RENEAU: Can you tell me?

BUNDY: Oh yes. Oh, excuse me. Uh … madness, what can I say. It was, basically, to do what was done.

RENEAU: Where were you living at the time?

BUNDY: Salt Lake City.

RENEAU: Was that the purpose for your visit to the dormitory, the night you were asked to leave?

BUNDY: Well, not specifically. I mean it was … you have to… I'd have to do a lot of explaining if my explanations would do. It was more or less that it was some idle roaming around. It wasn't, it was non-specific, you know, for anything in particular.

RENEAU: Was there any sexual contact with either of these two girls?

BUNDY: Well, yes, I'm afraid there was, and yet I … you know…

RENEAU: As to both of the girls?

BUNDY: Yes.

RENEAU: Did you notice, as to either of these girls, any jewelry, or other items like that, they were wearing?

BUNDY: The only thing that comes to mind is with the second girl. Would be a kind of bead necklace, an old simple little bead necklace, that's all.

RENEAU: Do you recall what color it would have been?

BUNDY: Well, I'm not really good at describing jewelry and bead doesn't really describe it. They were more like long little spaghetti with a string struck through it and they were black and a lighter color.

RENEAU: What was done with that necklace?

BUNDY: I think it was left, that was left with the body.

RENEAU: Still on the body at the time it was placed in the river?

BUNDY: Yes.

RENEAU: Were either of these girls other than Caucasian?

BUNDY: No, they were both Caucasians.

RENEAU: All right now. This route, this is regarding incident number two where you picked up the hitchhiker near Boise. You had made this drive a number of times by then?

BUNDY: Yes.

RENEAU: On this route you have traveled a number of times. As you mentioned, it was under construction, parts of the road were under construction at the time. After leaving Boise in those years, there were a couple of different places on the way to Pocatello where it would turn into a two-lane highway. Do you recall, whether or not, this section where you had the river to your right might have been one of those?

BUNDY: No, I've wondered about that. I mean, as I traveled during that period when it went back and forth and when there was a part that was, during the mid-70's, '73,'74,'75, wait a minute … at least one part of it was a basically old style two-lane highway with telephone poles and all that, and even though it was night, it was pretty evident that when you go back to an old two-lane highway it's just a different way of driving, and it feels like I was back on that kind of stretch of roadway near the river.

RENEAU: During one of those stretches, during that period of time, one of the two-lane roads went through a very small town. Do you recall any buildings or anything like that before you got to the railroad trestle?

BUNDY: Well, let me think. I know the kind of place you're talking about and I can't say that I'm … that at that particular time that I can place going through a small town, as being near or before the area that I'm talking about.

RENEAU: Can you recall approximately how long it was, after you made the turn off you described, before you reached the river?

BUNDY: Oh, it was real near, real close by I mean, no more than just, you know, a minute or so.

RENEAU: When you parked the vehicle when you got down close to the river, did you have to park under or near the railroad trestle you described?

BUNDY: It seems to me that it was like a piece of roadway that kind of deadened heading downhill. Like there used to be an access road that had gone down to the river, but it sort of had been washed away, but it was near, it was maybe no more than forty ... thirty ... forty yards away from the trestle.

RENEAU: As to the first incident that you described, we talked about ... you said you thought that it might be about five miles outside of town that you drove to the point where you made the stop at the river. Can you tell us what the terrain, trees that kind of thing, were (sic) like around the spot where you placed the body in the river?

BUNDY: It was more than ... there was some vegetation at the river edge leading from the roadway to the river ... there was a grassy, it was grassy, there weren't any trees or anything. Above the roadway, away from the river, there was a hilly area, but again, no trees, no woodlands, and further down the way there was a bridge, not an old bridge, but a small, uh ... just a very small, it may have even been a one-lane bridge, but it was conceivable it was two-lane, but I don't remember, that I went across it, but I did note that, maybe two hundred yards downstream.

RENEAU: Can you recall how wide the river was at that point?

BUNDY: At that time, it seemed like it was in flood stage. I mean, it seemed like it was up above its banks and ...

RENEAU: Can you recall at that point the approximate distance between the banks?

BUNDY: Ya, I'm trying, uh ... let's see, it's not real wide like I know the Snake can be ... it's a hundred yards.

RENEAU: Was there a road that led right to the spot where you stopped?

BUNDY: No, no, the road was maybe 50 yards away from, well it was, ya, there was no roadway. The paved road ran maybe about 50 yards away. And then, there was what looked like a kind of area where people would drive down but not enough to make a roadway, you know what I'm saying? Just sort of an obvious turn off kind of place but where people might stop and go fishing, but where there wasn't a road or anything formal.

RENEAU: When you left Pocatello headed north, were you on the freeway at that time?

BUNDY: I believe so, yes.

RENEAU: Perhaps if we could look at the map and that portion. All right, we can see there where the ... so, you'd be en route to Blackfoot if you were on the freeway.

BUNDY: It's what it looks like but it doesn't look like... I didn't think it would be that far because we're talking in mileage terms like twenty-one miles. Which one of these dots... is this Pocatello?

RENEAU: Up to the north, a little further right, before you see where it says Chubbuck. That whole area immediate (sic) south of Chubbuck is Pocatello.

BUNDY: Okay. Well then, I don't know, that's an awful long distance but it don't (sic) ...this is a reservoir obviously here, right?

RENEAU: Yes.

BUNDY: Okay, well, all I know is the freeway, I do know my recollection was that the freeway was ... I took an off-ramp then went left or west of the freeway, so that much I...

RENEAU: Do you recall passing the Indian Reservation or

some factories?

BUNDY: No.

RENEAU: But you did take an off-ramp?

BUNDY: Yes.

RENEAU: And that led you to another paved road, which went down to the river or close to the river and then stopped?

BUNDY: Went alongside the river and at some point part of it branched across the small bridge south of this location we're talking about. I didn't come to the end of it, I mean the paved road itself.

RENEAU: And the bridge would have been to your south?

BUNDY: Well, ya, if the way this river's running, ya, it would have been downstream.

RENEAU: Did you see anyone else around the area on your approach down there?

BUNDY: As a matter of fact, well, I heard some kids, I assumed it to be kids I didn't see, catch a glimpse of them, riding dirt bikes on this hilly area that was above the roadway away from the river.

RENEAU: Did it look like that was an area commonly used for that purpose?

BUNDY: It struck me that it was, yes.

RENEAU: What time of day was this by the time that this occurred, by the time you reached the river, excuse me?

BUNDY: Three o'clock.

RENEAU: After you left the junior high school, where did

you go from there?

BUNDY: Uh, back to the Holiday Inn.

RENEAU: Is that where the sexual contact occurred?

BUNDY: Well, that's when I have a hard time talking about some of these things.

RENEAU: Do you recall if you had to go to the desk or get a key?

BUNDY: No.

RENEAU: Do you recall what part of the Holiday Inn you were staying?

BUNDY: Yes.

RENEAU: Can you describe for me, from the entrance, approximately where your room would have been?

BUNDY: It was all the way around what I would call the back, the far side from the desk, the main entrance, then all the around the back side, so you drive basically all the way around to the back. You know, you'd have to take a circuitous route around the, the various wings of the Holiday Inn to get around to the back side of it, and it would've been the first floor, I mean the ground level.

RENEAU: Did you keep any items involving either of these incidents for any purpose?

BUNDY: No, I didn't.

RENEAU: When we talked about the backpack, you said that it was thrown in a real dumpsite. Do you ...

BUNDY: Well, ya, I should say, how to describe this place

this is an area south of Salt Lake City where there are lots of illegal dumping and there's also a general area where the real city dump, at least used to be before the lake rose (sic), I guess, and because a lot of the garbage trucks took that route, there was lots of stuff along the sides of the highways so, you know, it was hardly noticeable, what else was out there. So, it was just a lot of things laying all around the roadway and then off the road there were a lot of illegal dump sites. People did a lot of dumping.

RENEAU: In addition to the instances that you described for us, did you ... were there ever any unsuccessful attempts in Idaho, specifically around the Pocatello area?

BUNDY: No, oh, oh, wait a minute, ya, I should just give that a little bit more thought, I could have. I thought you meant before, on that particular trip, which was the only trip that I made to Pocatello from Salt Lake.

RENEAU: There weren't any unsuccessful ones in Pocatello that you recall?

BUNDY: No, not really, no.

RENEAU: Is there anything that might have been reported?

BUNDY: Again, only that incident on the college campus would conceivably have been reported and I'm not so sure about that.

RENEAU: This green backpack ... could you describe for me some of the other contents besides the identification? If you recall?

MS. WEINER: We're done. Our hour is up.

BUNDY: See what you ... you know, I don't need to tell you your job, but if you come up with questions that are important, that you simply want me to answer, perhaps I can find a way to do that. I know this isn't much time.

RENEAU: I'd appreciate that very much. Naturally, we're going to start checking right away on some of this information and we may very well have more questions later.

The Florida Reports

Detective Don Patchen, lead investigator in the Chi Omega case in Tallahassee, Florida. Patchen, who had a lunch meeting scheduled with the governor of Florida on the day Bundy was put to death, quickly cancelled when he received, and accepted, an invitation to attend the killer's execution Courtesy Don Patchen

Author's note: What follows are reports from the Tallahassee Police Department detailing Ted Bundy's sojourn into the state of Florida after his second successful escape from his captors in Colorado. When he arrived in the city, he headed for his favorite location: The university district of Florida State University. Not only could he identify with the academic atmosphere, but the university district also offered him an array of college coeds, and no matter what other locations in which Bundy decided to kill, the college campus would remain his most loved spot to hunt and kill young women.

Bundy took the name Chris Hagen, and with what little money he had left from his escape, he secured a room at The Oak, at 409 West College Avenue, very close to the university. It was a rather large structure, actually bigger than it looked from the outside front of the building, and Bundy had a second-floor apartment. Just like its name emblazoned above the front door suggests, there was a very large oak tree in the front yard.

Of course, no one recognized him, and he kept a somewhat low profile among the other residents. For a time, Bundy would go about his business and his normal routine of stealing whatever he needed from the unsuspecting victims who left their wallets or purses unattended. The first report will give the reader a partial listing of Bundy's shopping tastes, items he often purchased with other people's money. But that need to kill; that diabolical craving to destroy the female of the species, would begin to arise again in the killer, and when that occurred, Tallahassee's time of fear and suffering began.

What follows are several reports, beginning with the items Ted Bundy purchased with stolen credit cards. Following these are reports from the officers who responded to the carnage at the Chi Omega sorority house at approximately 3:30 a.m. on February 15, 1978, after Bundy had savagely attacked a number of coeds, killing two. The first report is from Officer Henry Winkler, after he arrived on the scene following the initial patrol cars and EMTs who responded to the original call.

EVIDENCE:

Exhibit 27: VISA credit card charge on Labadie card taken by Mark Barlow at the Tallassee Hilton. The transaction took place February 3, 1978, in the amount of $21.40, Mr. Barlow lists his address as 441 Chapel Hill Drive, Apartment 114, Tallahassee.

Exhibit 28: VISA charge on Labadie VISA card at the WHERE? Still Tallahassee? Hilton, taken by Beverly Frank, on February 1, 1978, in the amount of $4.45. Ms. Franks lists her address as P.O. Box 2604, Tallahassee Florida. This writer has not interviewed any of the witnesses at the Hilton.

Exhibit 29: ?? was taken by an unknown employee on February 1, 1978, in the amount of $16.74. This writer has not interviewed any witness at the Hilton.

Exhibit 32: Mastercharge charge at the Andrews 2nd Act on the account of William R. Evans taken by Jean Bodon, dated February 5, 1978, in the amount of $19.60. Mr. Bodon remembers and can identify the defendant.

Exhibit 33: TYPE OF CHARGE was taken by a Mr. Zami who works at the deli on Adams Street. At the time this writer received the receipt, Mr. Zami was not working. His current address is not known at this time. The purchase was dated January 28, 1978, in the amount of $14.48.

Exhibit 34: Evans Charge transaction taken by Brenda Cross on XX Date, while she was working at the Tasty Pastry Bakery, for the purchase of cookies, in the amount of $8.58.

Ms. Cross stated she remembered the defendant when she saw the photos in the paper. The defendant came in twice, the first time he forgot the credit card. Ms. Cross's parents own the bakery at Timberline Shop on the Square.

The following two charges involve the William R. Evans account.

Exhibit 1: J. Byron's Department Store, February 6, 1978, taken by Pat Elston. Ms. Elston does remember the transaction for $8.32 and it was for pajamas.

Exhibit 2: was taken by Marilyn Shear Also at J. Byron's, taken by Marilyn Shear, on XX date, in the amount of XX, for the purchase of XX. Her address is unknown at this time. This writer has attempted to locate her but has been unsuccessful.

Exhibit 3: this transaction was taken by Mrs. Louise Bennett while she worked at Shaw's. Mrs. Bennett's current address is….Mrs. Bennett remembers selling him bath accessories but that was all she could remember.

Exhibit 4: This transaction was taken by Jean Olsheski while she worked at Richards Luggage on College Avenue. A call was placed to authorization, who okayed the purchase. It is possible this item was located at the time Bundy was arrested, but to date I have not seen a complete inventory list.

Exhibit 5: this transaction was taken by Elizabeth Adkinson at Rapp's Racquet Shop on Park Avenue. She could not identify the suspect. She was comparing the invoice to the photos of the defendant from the paper.

Exhibit 6: this transaction was taken by Elizabeth Adkinson also. This transaction was taken the day after exh.5, she could not remember Bundy.

Exhibits 7 and 8: were transactions taken by an employee at Clyde's, the employee is not known. The company Clyde's is imprinted on the receipts.

Exhibit 9: is a transaction taken by Charles Degal while he was employed at the Tallahassee Hilton. It was taken 4 February 78, in the amount of $4.14.

Exhibit 10: is another transaction taken at the Tallahassee Hilton. The person who took the transaction is not known since the employee did not sign the invoice.

Exhibit 11: This transaction was taken by Raymond Brown at Eckerd's in the Northwood Mall. Mr. Brown could not remember what was purchased.

RECOMMENDED DISPOSITION:

Closed cleared by arrest of Ted Bundy.

Total arrests: 11

Total charges: 22

Author's note: What follows are the reports from the Tallassee PD pertaining to Chi Omega murders and reports from the Lake City PD covering the murder of Kimberly Leach.

VICTIM: Bowman, Margaret

Refer to cases; M-1594, Lisa Levy, Homicide; M-1595, Karen Chandler, Assault; M-1596, Kathy Kleiner, Assault.

This writer was dispatched to 661 W. Jefferson Street, Chi Omega Sorority House, at approximately 3:30 a.m. on January 15, 1978, to assist in a crime scene investigation.

This writer met with officer Henry Newkirk and Investigator Don Patchen, both of Tallahassee Police Department, and was directed to the second floor, rooms #4, #8, and #9 where the assaults had taken place.

This writer first entered room #9 and observed the body of Margaret Bowman W/F, lying face down with her head pointed in a southerly direction and her feet pointed toward the north. She was lying partially on the right side of her face. The body in place and the entire room were photographed. Her hands were then placed in paper bags and the body was transported to T.M.H. (*Author's note: Tallahassee Memorial Hospital*) by Culley Funeral Home. This writer then proceeded to room #8 and observed blood on both beds. Blood was also located on walls around both beds and on the ceiling between the windows and light fixture. These blood splatters were photographed. Blood was also located on the intercom button located on the east wall just inside the entrance door. This blood along with both beds and the entire room were photographed.

This writer observed several teeth on the right bed in room #8 (Kleiner). The bed linens with the teeth were collected from both beds in room #8.

This writer then entered room #4, the room of Lisa Levy, and observed blood on the victim's bed. Photographs were taken of this blood and the entire room.

Bark of unknown type was located on the floor and beds in all three rooms (#4, #8, #9), and this bark was collected.

This writer was assisted in processing and collecting evidence from the scene by Officer Oscar Brannon, Tallahassee Police Department and Deputy Carroll Hurdle, Leon County Sherriff's Office.

This writer transported the evidence to T.P.D. lab and placed it in a locked area.

This writer then proceeded to the TMH morgue and met with Investigator Sam Boykin, T.P.D., and Sheriff Ken Katsaris. This writer photographed the body of victim Lisa Levy. Photographs taken are as follows: a bruise on right shoulder; teeth marks on right breast and left buttock; legs; overall body. A sexual assault kit was used on the victim to collect blood; pubic and head hair; fingernail scrapings; vaginal swabs; and saliva for examination by the crime lab. This writer rolled inked finger and palm impressions of the victim, and observed the autopsy performed by Dr. Woods (see pathologist's report).

This writer then photographed the victim, Margaret Bowman. Photographs taken are as follows: abrasion mark upper left leg; head wounds; and overall body. A sexual assault kit was used on victim to collect blood; pubic and head hair; fingernail scrapings; vaginal swabs; and saliva for examination by the crime lab. This writer rolled inked ginger and palm impressions on victim, and observed the autopsy performed by Dr. Woods (see pathologist's report).

Author's note: The following report is from Officer Henry Newkirk, of the Tallassee PD:

This writer arrived at 661 W. Jefferson St. at approximately 3:35 am. Once upstairs in the east west hallway this writer observed T.M.H. E.M.T.s attending to Lisa Levy in room #4; Karen Chandler in room #3, and Katherine Kleiner in room #8. Both Karen and Katherine showed evidence of having been beaten severely about the head and face. Lisa Levy appeared to be lifeless as E.M. T.s performed C.P.R.

At this time, the writer turned his attention to trying to

organize the other ladies in the hallway into one room so as to quell some of the extraneous wandering and commotion. Once inside the room this writer began questioning the girls as to anything they saw or heard. At this time a Melanie Nelson (661 W. Jefferson St.) approached this writer and asked that I look into room #9 to make sure Margaret Bowman was all right since she had not exited her room. This writer entered room #9 and immediately closed the door behind me once I observed blood on a pillow. Ms. Bowman was lying on the bed in the south-west corner of the room with her head and feet pointing in the south-north direction, respectively. The bedspread was covering Ms. Bowman's entire body with the exception of her head – which was tilted to the right lying on her pillow. (Her face was facing the west wall). This writer pulled back the cover (bedspread) and observed Ms. Bowman had been strangled with a nylon panty hose. Her legs were bent outwardly and spread open. (Note: Ms. Bowman was lying on her stomach.) Her right arm was extended down her side and her left arm was bent with her elbow facing east and her left hand resting on her back. Both palms of the hands were turned inward. This writer turned Ms. Bowman over onto her right side to check for a heartbeat or pulse and discovered neither. This writer looked at Ms. Bowman's head and observed where Ms. Bowman had received a crushing blow to her right forehead coupled with what appeared to be two puncture wounds in the same vicinity. Massive bleeding occurred from both the forehead and the right ear, with clotting occurring in the right ear. Additionally Ms. Bowman's neck appeared to be disjointed leading this writer to believe there was a possible neck fracture. Ms. Bowman's body was relatively warm to the touch and her eyes were glassy with pupils dilated.

This writer observed Ms. Bowman was wearing a yellow

nitie (sic) with no panties and had a thin gold chain around her neck. This writer covered Ms. Bowman with the bedspread and in so doing noticed bark particles both on the bed and on the floor. There was no evidence of a struggle either on the bed or in the room. The room was not ransacked and at this writing nothing was known to be missing.

This writer then exited the room and notified Officer Brannon and F.S.U. officers whereupon a complete search was undertaken of the house. Room #9 was sealed off and secured...

This writer returned to the room where I originally placed the ladies and began questioning Ms. Nelson. Ms. Nelson stated that she came in house from a date at 2:15 a.m. and noticed that the rear door was unlocked; however, she did not mention it to anyone. Ms. Bowman walked downstairs to see Ms. Nelson, whereupon they both walked back upstairs and into Ms. Bowman's room. They talked until 2:40 a.m. when Ms. Nelson returned to her room and left Ms. Bowman alone as her roommate was (is) out of town. Ms. Nelson did not observe anything unusual with the exception of the unlocked door.

Ms. Carol Johnson, 661 W. Jefferson St. was not interviewed, however, she did state the rear door was unlocked at 3:00 a.m. when she came home – did not notice anything else significant. Ms. Terri Murphy stated the door was locked at 2:35 a.m. when she came home and she pulled the door tight behind her. These girls' room #s were not ascertained nor were their proximity to room #'s #3, 4, 8, & 9. All the girls collectively stated they did not see or hear anything unusual.

Culley's funeral home picked up Ms. Bowman's body and this writer accompanied them to the T.M.H. morgue. This writer can testify that the body was not disturbed in any way prior to autopsy.

This writer observed both autopsies at T.M.H. performed by Dr. Wood (pathologist).

Note this writer searched the immediate the grounds around the house for possible physical evidence but failed to find any viable …

Author's note: What follows is a partial listing of residents who were living at 409 W. College Avenue at the same time that Bundy was living there. All names used are correct, but I will not be adding dates of birth for obvious reasons. Any interactions with Bundy, as he went about using the alias "Chris Hagen," are also included.

- Philip Nicholas Tortorcini, 409 W. College Ave. Apt. #4, FSU Student, cannot recall Chris Hagen

- Jadon Menear, 409 W. College Ave. Apt. #5, does not recall Chris Hagen

- Charles Orville Peak, 409 W. College Ave. Apt. M-5

- Terry Cox, 409 W. College Ave. Apt. L-5, FSU Student and employed by Fla. Dept. of Commerce

- Susie Roos, 409 W. College Ave. Apt. #7, FSU Student, Ms. Roos stated that she had only spoken to Chris M. Hagen in passing (i.e., hello, good morning.)

- Roger Francis Mueller, 409 W. College Ave. Apt. #8, Mr. Mueller cannot recall Chris M. Hagen

- Benjamin Arnold Masterson, 409 W. College Ave. Apt. #13, He has talked with Mr. Hagen several times. He has seen Mr. Hagen on a 10 speed bike. Has seen Mr. Hagen with Francine Messier on occasions. Has seen Mr. Hagen around 1:00 a.m. jogging and or riding his bicycle on different occasions, but cannot remember what dates

- Tina Louise Hopkins, 409 W. College Ave. Apt. #14, TCC Student, (see attached statement Clark/West)

- Earl Don Ramsey, Jr., 409 W. College Ave. Apt. #11, works Wakulla Co. Newspaper 984-5554 (See recorded statement Clark/West)

- Yong H Hyon, 409 W. College Ave. Apt. #16, FSU Student (See recorded statement Clark/West)

- Frances Messier, 409 W. College Ave. Apt. #18, Lively Vo-Tech & TCC Student. (See recorded statement Clark/West)

- Robert Hill Fulford, Jr, 415 W. College Ave. Owner/Manager of the Oaks, 409 W. College Ave. (See recorded statement Clark/West/ 2-17-78)

Author's note: After the killings at Chi Omega, Bundy attacked Cheryl Thomas at her Dunwoody apartment only blocks from Chi Omega. He entered through a window, and catching her in bed, he beat her about the head with the same log he'd previously used at the sorority house. His intention was to strangle her while having sex with her from behind, but because of Cheryl's persistent neighbor, Debbie Ciccarelli, Bundy was forced to cut short his attack. Debbie, with whom Cheryl shared space in the duplex, kept calling her phone and beating on the wall, after hearing sounds like pounding noises and someone crying coming from her apartment. After relieving himself through masturbation,

Bundy hurried back out the same way he had entered.

After Bundy escaped from his second crime scene of the night, he headed back to College Avenue. What follows is from my book The Bundy Murders: A Comprehensive History: "According to later testimony by Russell Gage and Henry Palumbo, who returned to The Oak sometime after 4:00 a.m., they found 'Chris' standing on the front porch of the rooming house, staring blankly towards the university. When they said hello to him, he did not answer. Gage told the jury that Bundy joined a group of residents just a short time later to discuss the Chi Omega murders, news of which was now being heard over the Tallahassee radio stations. Gage said that Bundy made a statement that "this was probably a professional job, and this guy has done it before (p. 207)."

After the murders at Chi Omega, Bundy's thirst for blood was satiated for a while. Once that need arose again, he headed out of Tallahassee in a stolen FSU media van (he had keys made to the vehicle prior to stealing it), and drove to Jacksonville, Florida, where he intended to kill again. However, he was unsuccessful in Jacksonville, despite all his activity there. His next (and last) victim was twelve-year-old Kimberly Diane Leach, of Lake City, Florida. Having abducted the young girl, while she was crossing the school grounds going from one building to another, Bundy stopped the van (blocking traffic) and led her to the passenger side of the vehicle. He then took her some forty miles away, raped and murdered her (he cut her throat with a knife), and left her body under a small tin hog shed.

What follows is from a report contained within the court records:

On February 9, 1978, Kimberly Diane Leach, aged 12, was

driven to the Lake City Junior High School, located on Duval Street (U.S. Highway 90), Lake City, Columbia County, Florida, by her mother, Freda Leach, at approximately 8:00 a.m. (R. 3865) It was a cold, rainy morning (R. 3989).

After chatting with some school friends, the Leach girl went to her homeroom class at approximately 8:30 a.m. (R. 3899). Her homeroom class was located in the Central Building (R. 3957). Her homeroom teacher was John Lawrence Bishop. After approximately fifteen minutes of attendance, the school bell rang for the first period class, which for the Leach girl was physical education. Because of the inclement weather, students assembled in the auditorium to watch a movie, as opposed to going outside to play. (R. 3944).

For the Leach girl to get from her homeroom classroom in the Central Building to the auditorium, she had to exit the rear of the school building, go outside, walk around some portable buildings, and across the basketball courts (R. 3910), a total distance of approximately 247 feet, to enter the auditorium. (R.6432). After she had departed the classroom, Mr. Bishop noticed that she had left her purse behind. He then dispatched a classmate, Tandy Bonner, to the auditorium to bring Leach back to her homeroom classroom to retrieve her purse (R. 3919). Leach did, in fact, leave the auditorium with the permission of her Physical Education teacher, Mrs. Juanita Caldwell, and returned to Mr. Bishop's classroom and got her purse (R.3943).

When she exited her original homeroom classroom to return to the auditorium, it was approximately 9:20 to 9:25 a.m. (R. 13878) This was the last time that anyone could positively identify having seen Kimberly Diane Leach until her remains were found in a tin hog shed located in Suwannee County, Florida, approximately 35 to 40 miles west of Lake City

Junior High School (R. 4236).

There was no report of a "positive" identification of having seen the Leach girl after her disappearance until five months, three weeks and two days later (R. 4074). On the day of her disappearance, as testified to by her mother, the Leach girl was wearing Hush Puppies shoes, white cotton socks, blue denim jeans, a blue football type jersey pullover shirt with the number 83 emblazoned in red on the front, a three-quarter length fur-trimmed coat, and she was carrying a denim purse (R. 3877).

At approximately 2:30 p.m. that day, the Leach girl's parents were contacted by the school officials and informed that she had not attended her second period and subsequent class periods (R. 3875, 3882).

A search of the school grounds and the school's buildings were made and she was not found. The police were called in and began their investigation (R. 3883).

On February 11, 1978, a picture of Kimberly Diane Leach, her description, and facts of her disappearance appeared in the local and state news media, both press and television (R. 5773). Over the course of the next several months, a search in extent and intensity virtually unheard of in the annals of Florida history was conducted to locate her (R. 17522-14529, 4257).

A task force, totaling some one hundred members at any one time, was amassed, and virtually every inch of ground in Columbia County and surrounding counties, was covered by the search party (R. 4238, 4258).

On April 7, 1978, (R. 4231) while part of the search party searched a wooded area near the Suwannee River in

Suwannee County, Florida, one of the members of the search party, Florida Highway Patrol Trooper Kenneth W. Robinson stumbled upon a tin hog shed. Upon bending down and peering therein, he saw remains of a human body and pile of clothes (R. 4234-4235). Trooper Robinson then summoned the other members of the search party (R. 4235). The area was cordoned off to await the arrival of the State Medical Examiner and Anthropologist, the Florida Department of Law Enforcement Crime Lab Team, members of the State's Attorney's Office, and the investigators in charge of the disappearance of Kimberly Diane Leach (R. 4250).

During the course of the search and investigation, untold numbers of persons were questioned with regard to the disappearance. Numerous reports of sightings of the Leach girl were made to the task force, but none proved fruitful (R. 5775). Requests for information was (sic) made almost daily over the radio and television stations. Almost daily pleas were made in the Press for information from anyone who might have any knowledge concerning the disappearance of Kimberly Diane Leach, and for any such persons to please come forward. Fliers containing her picture, her name, her description, the description of her clothing, were printed and posted in conspicuous places all over Columbia, County, Florida, and in particular, at the Police Department located in the same building with the Lake City Fire Department (R. 4142).

Where was Kimberly Leach Killed?

In my book, The Bundy Murders, I say that Bundy killed Kim Leach while raping her (from behind) while inside the hog shed in which she was ultimately found, and that he killed her by slashing at her throat with a hunting knife he'd recently purchased. *I came to this conclusion based on the available evidence in the record, and the recorded statements of those who were close to the case: well-informed individuals, and those who would have the most definitive and trustworthy answers. From everything that I researched, the van did not contain the amount of blood necessary that would lead one to think such a ghastly murder had been committed there. As we shall see, there was some evidence in a recorded statement that she may have been killed where her body was found- the hog shed- and this is the theory I finally went with for the book.*

In 2015, and again in 2016, a number of people who had read my book, The Bundy Murders, contacted me about what I'd said in my book concerning where Leach was murdered, versus what has been conveyed in one of the more recent books about Ted Bundy, and how the two theories are complete opposites. In that particular book, I was informed that the writer maintains that Bundy did, in fact, kill Kim in the van, due to the amount of blood found inside the vehicle.

Well, I thought, those two theories are opposites indeed, and I wondered what the author might have discovered that I had missed? Or, I thought, perhaps there is new evidence, however unlikely that is. I knew, as far as I could tell, that nothing in the official record that I'd read pointed definitively either way; except that it seemed most likely he killed her while inside the hog shed. Still, to my knowledge, there was no way to conclusively prove either theory. Finally, after I began my research for this, my third and last Bundy book, I found the following information, reprinted from newspapers from the time, quoting the medical examiner and the prosecuting attorney, Bob Dekle:

January 24, 1980

ORLANDO, Fla. A medical examiner testified Wednesday at the Theodore Bundy trial that 12-year-old Kimberly Leach was probably killed during sexual intercourse at an abandoned North Florida hog shed 35 miles from where she disappeared.

There was also this taken from the Salt Lake Tribune of April 9, 1978:

LIVE OAK, Fla.

Dekle said investigators did not know whether the girl died where she was found or if her body was taken there. "We really don't know. We've got some theories about it, but all they are is theories." he said.

Although this statement from Dekle was given just two days after Kim's body was located, it's nearly two months after the discovery of the van on February 13th. As such, there was plenty of time, in my view, to determine whether or not the Leach girl died in the van, and yet they were still unsure. Because of what the ME said, I still believe the most likely site of Kim's murder was in the hog shed. Of course, I can't be dogmatic about it, and I'd be perfectly happy to change my opinion if I saw evidence that conclusively points to the van as being the scene of the murder. Until that day, a day that may never arrive, I will maintain that what I have written in <u>The Bundy Murders</u> is the correct answer.

Author's note: Bundy, who was arrested in Pensacola, Florida, in the early morning hours of February 15, 1978 (exactly one month after the Chi Omega murders), after he was spotted trolling the city in a stolen VW, had been in custody over six weeks by the time the remains of Kimberly

Leach were found. Of course, investigators understood Bundy was her killer, but getting him to admit it just wasn't going to happen. He would, however, vaguely allude to it in a deposition he conducted (Bundy was again acting as his own attorney) with Detective Norman Chapman during his trial for her murder. Here is a portion of that transcript:

Q: To the best of your recollection, Officer Chapman, what was it you recall Theodore Bundy saying about the Kimberly Leach case that I referred to earlier? You recall the exact words? You recall your question? Let's go back, and see if I understand what you said. You were questioning Mr. Bundy about the location of Kimberly Leach.

A: I asked Mr. Bundy, we were talking about certain things, and I asked Mr. Bundy, I told him and I said, "Ted, I will go," to the best of my knowledge, "and locate the girl, find the body and let her parents know where she's at"; and Mr. Bundy replied that "I cannot do that to you because the site is too horrible to look at."

What follows is a Q & A that Liz Kloepfer had with Detective Bob Keppel and Major Nick Mackie on February 21, 1978. Bundy had telephoned Liz soon after his arrest in Pensacola. Although the interviewee's name is redacted, it is Liz Kloepfer:

Case 75-29267

The date is 2-21-78. The time is 1520 hours. This will be an interview with (redacted). Those present at the interview are: (redacted), Major Nick Mackie, and Detective Robert Keppel.

Keppel: Are you aware that this interview is being taped?

Redacted: Yes.

Keppel: Is it taped with your approval?

Redacted: Yes.

Keppel: Okay. Would you begin on February 16, 1978, about 5:00 a.m. on Thursday, and describe a telephone call that you received from Ted Bundy.

Redacted: Yes. It was 5:00 p.m. on Thursday.

Keppel: 5:00 p.m.?

Redacted: Yes.

Keppel: Okay.

Redacted: And he called collect and my daughter accepted the charges. I told him that he shouldn't be calling me, that my phone had a trap on it, and he said he was in custody. I asked him, "Where?" And he said, "Florida." And later in the conversation, he said, he repeated over and over again, that this was really going to be bad when it broke, that it wasn't going to break until tomorrow morning in the press but it was going to be really ugly. I asked him if he was referring to the murders of some sorority girls in Florida. And he said that he wouldn't talk about it. And I told him that I had asked an FBI agent about those murders up here 'cause I was concerned about them. And he didn't want to talk about it. And, uh, then in the conversation he told me that he wished that we could sit down and talk about things, without anyone listening, about why he was the way he is, and I said, "Are you telling me that you are sick?" And he said, he was very defensive, and he told me to back off, and what he was referring to was how come he had hurt me so many times.

Keppel: Did you ask him any specific questions?

Redacted: I asked him how he had been taken into custody.

Keppel: Did he answer you?

Redacted: Not that night. He did the next night.

Keppel: Okay.

Redacted: We talked for about an hour. On Thursday. And then he was going to hang up and call his mother and call back, and when he called back we didn't accept charges and then we took the phone off the hook. Then the next Saturday morning at 2:00 he called again, collect, and he said he wanted to talk about what we'd been talking about in the first phone call. And I said: "You mean about being sick?" And he said: "Yes." Then he said that he was going to try to clear things up in a way that he could be back in Washington close to his family… that he … I can't remember exactly how he got into talking about it ... the crimes … he told me that he was sick and that he was consumed by something that he didn't understand and that, uh, that he just couldn't contain it, uh, I asked him – oh, go ahead.

Keppel: Did he mention why he couldn't contain it?

Redacted: Well, he said that he tried, he said that it took so much of his time, and that's why he wasn't doing well in law school, and that he couldn't seem to get his act together, because he spent so much time trying to maintain a normal life and he just couldn't do it, he said that he was preoccupied with this force. Ah, he told me that, I asked him if I somehow played a part in what had happened, and he said that no, for years before he even met me he'd been fighting the same sickness and that when it broke we just happened to be together. Uh, he mentioned an incident about following a sorority girl, uh, he didn't do anything that night, but uh, he just told me that's how it was, he was out late at night and he would just follow people like that, but that he'd try not to but he just did it anyway. Uh …

Keppel: Did he mention anything to do with sorority girls at the University of Washington?

Redacted: Well, this incident did take place on campus, where he followed this girl, he didn't talk about the girl who was abducted from there. Uh, he did talk about Lake Sammamish, he told me that he was, he started by saying that he was sick, and he said: "I don't have a split personality, and I don't have blackouts." He said: "I remember everything I've done." And he mentioned the day, July 14th, when two women were abducted from Lake Sammamish and we went out to eat that night about 5:00 and he was saying that he remembered that he ate two hamburgers and he enjoyed every bite of it. And that we went to Ferrell's after and he said that it wasn't that he had forgotten what he'd done that day or that he couldn't remember, but just said that it was over.

Keppel: The incident was over?

Redacted: Yeah, that's the implication I got.

Keppel: Did he mention the incident specifically?

Redacted; Yes.

Keppel: What did he say?

Redacted: He just mentioned the day. He didn't …

Keppel: He mentioned July 14th?

Redacted: He said, "The day of Lake Sammamish."

Keppel: "The day of Lake Sammamish" is what he said?

Redacted: Uh huh. Uh …

Keppel: Did he specifically say that he had done something to some women that day?

Redacted: No. No. I knew what he was talking about, and he knew that I knew it, so he didn't relay any … uh, he said that he would answer any questions that he could, and I asked him about the night that Brenda Ball disappeared because he'd been with me and my family and he'd left early in the evening and then the next day was late to my daughter's baptism and I asked him if that's where he'd been, and he mumbled something and I couldn't understand the answer and then he said, "It's pretty scary, isn't it?" And I said: "Yeah." (laugh) I asked him if he'd ever try to kill me and he told me that at one incident that he did.

Keppel: What was that?

Redacted: Oh, he used to sleep in a hide-a-bed by the fireplace in the living room and he closed the damper – I was drunk that night – and he closed the damper, put towels under the door and then he left. Then he told me that he'd been really trying hard to control this sickness and that he'd been staying off the streets and trying to be normal and that it just happened that I was there when he felt it coming on and that he wanted to kill me that night.

Keppel: What steps did he take to either attempt to kill you or not to kill you?

Redacted: Well, I guess he was just going to let me die of smoke inhalation, I guess. He did tell me, I woke up briefly, and he said, "I'm going to go home and get my fan, the fireplace is backed up." And he left and he didn't come back.

Keppel: Do you recall what night that was? What period of time?

Redacted: I think it was the Fall of '73.

Keppel: The Fall of '73?

Redacted: I think so.

Keppel: Did he mention the specific time that he coordinated with you, the time of your meeting to any of this starting, or had it started prior to meeting you?

Redacted: Well, I asked him. I told him that the police were talking about murders that had happened since 1969, and I said, "That's the year we met each other." And I asked him what I had to do with this whole thing? And he said, "Nothing," that he'd been trying to control it for years and that, uh, that we just happened to be together when it got the best of him. He told me, I told him, when we were talking about 1969 being the starting date, he said that the police were years off and he talked about, I believe he said that during '71, and '72, and '73 it was taking up more of his time, time that he should have been using for other things. He told me that it wasn't me, that it was him that was sick, that it wasn't anything I'd done. Uh, I asked him, I mentioned that there was a phone call that he made to me from Salt Lake City when a woman down there was abducted. It was late at night and I've always thought, well, he couldn't be out abducting women because I'd talked to him on the phone that night, and I asked him if he didn't sometime call me or come over to touch base with reality after he had done some of these things, and he said, "That's a pretty good guess."

Author's note: Over the years, I've had certain people accuse me of adding things to my books which were not part of the record, and they have always been incorrect. . I don't blame them, as it usually stems from a common and basic lack of knowledge of the case on their part, and nothing more. While I have never felt the need to publish any of these odd occurrences, I will do so now in this one instance, given the type of vitriol from the individual accompanying the charge, and my momentary lapse of memory of where exactly within the record the passage exists, which would absolutely prove my point and forever vindicate me as to why I said what I said. So, without further delay, here is the gist of it.

When Bundy kidnapped Debra Kent from Viewmont High School in Bountiful, Utah, he rushed with the unconscious Debra Kent (he had whacked her in the head with a crowbar) to his apartment at 565 First Avenue. With Kent in a semicoma, he left her covered up in his VW, went upstairs, and called Liz. Of course, a small part may have been to create an alibi, but that, in my view, was not the principal reason for the call. His reason for the call, as I suggested in The Bundy Murders, "was his way of stepping back from the crevasse of complete insanity. It was a clear attempt to connect with the only real anchor to the normal world he possessed." Now, when this individual read this (he was working on a Bundy project), he accused me of making "shit (his word, not mine) up as I go along" and ridiculed me for it. Of course, I knew better, and I let him know there were so many things about the case that he didn't know. However, at the time, I couldn't remember exactly where in the record this passage lay hidden, so I responded with something else in that story that, in my view, proves my point. But lo and behold, when I was researching for this new book, I came across the statement from Liz above about her feeling that Ted would contact her after doing these things, as a way to, as she said, "touch base with reality." Bundy had all but agreed with her. With this, I consider the case now closed.

Keppel: Did he mention any other specific cases besides Brenda Ball and Lake Sammamish? Like, did he mention a Central Washington State College, or an Ellensburg, Oregon State University girl?

Redacted: No.

Keppel: Did any other missing girls or deaths come up other than those two?

Redacted: No.

Keppel: Did he mention anything with Utah or Colorado?

Redacted: No. Well, he alluded to Tallahassee. I asked him specifically about the Florida murders. And he told me that he didn't want to talk about them, but then in the phone conversation he said that he felt like he had a disease like alcoholism or something like alcoholics that couldn't take another drink, and he told me that it was just something that he couldn't be around and he knew it now. And I asked him what that was and he said: "Don't make me say it."

Keppel: Are there any other questions that you asked him on the Saturday conversation?

Redacted: Not that I can remember.

Keppel: Can you think of anything else that she hasn't covered?

Major: That's about it. That she repeated everything over again after he had said something to her, then she said: 'You said this?' 'At Lake Sammamish' 'You remember eating hamburgers?' 'You remember they tasted good?' And then you went to the other girl in south Seattle. And talking about that.

Keppel: Didn't you mention at all anything like ... I recall you saying before that he hadn't changed either a ski rack or a bicycle rack from his car to your car? Did he mention anything about that?

Redacted: No.

Keppel: And he really didn't say anything specific, like mention any names of girls. You were the one that mentioned the names. Right?

Redacted: Uh huh.

Keppel: Like Brenda Ball? He just brought up Lake Sammamish, right?

Redacted: Yes.

Keppel: Can you think of anything else she's covered before? This interview will be ended at 1533 hours, 2-21-78.

Author's Note: What follows are excerpts of interviews conducted by detectives with Tallassee PD with Kathy Kleiner and Karen Chandler of Chi Omega, and Cheryl Thomas, who was attacked at her Dunwoody apartment shortly after the Chi Omega murders. Their temporary mental confusion from the head injuries is quite obvious. Lastly, the transcriber has mistakenly used "MM" or "MMM" instead of the usual "Hmm". Because it's the official record I did not change it, but a word of explanation is in order.

Boykin: You probably don't remember we were talking to

you briefly the other morning, do you remember that?

Kleiner: MM

Boykin: I guess the nurses have told you we'd like to ask you a few questions. If possible, do you feel up to that?

Kleiner: If I can think.

Boykin: Okay. We sure need your help, if you will please. Uh, do you remember anything other than what you told us the other morning?

Kleiner: Indiscernible. (I heard a commotion, commotion.)

Boykin: You heard a commotion?

Kleiner: Susan Appleby and Jackie McGill, two sorority sisters, and a policeman.

Boykin: Can you describe any of the commotion for us?

Kleiner: (Indiscernible). Stuff like that.

Boykin: Did you see your assailant?

Kleiner: No, I didn't. (Indiscernible)

Boykin: Do you remember being struck?

Kleiner: No (indiscernible).

Nurse: You didn't feel anything?

Kleiner: Huh, uh.

Boykin: I thought you told us earlier you thought you were dreaming?

Kleiner: Yeah.

Boykin: Did you wake up in your bed?

Kleiner: No, (indiscernible).

Boykin: So when you woke up, the police officer was with you?

Kleiner: Yeah.

Clark: You don't remember anything prior to waking up and seeing your two sorority sisters and the police officer?

Kleiner: Huh, uh,I heard voices.I heard somebody's walkie-talkie.

Clark: Thank you very much Kathy, and we wish you luck, hurry up and get better all right, okay. Bye-bye.

Author's note: What follows is the testimony of Cheryl Thomas:

Boykin: How are you Ms. Thomas?

Thomas: (Indiscernible).

Boykin: I'm Investigator Boykin with the police department. And this is Investigator Clark with the sheriff's office. Wonder if you feel like trying to answer a few questions for us, maybe?

Thomas: I'll try but I don't think I can remember anything.

Boykin: Okay, now if you don't want to answer 'em or if you feel like you want to stop, just tell us, okay, and we'll leave, all right?

Thomas: MMM.

Boykin: Okay. Do you remember the man that assaulted

you?

Thomas: MMM.

Boykin: Could you remember if he were (sic) black or white?

Thomas: No.

Boykin: Okay, were you in your bed, uh, when this happened?

Thomas: Was I all by myself, I don't know, somebody must know.

Boykin: You were there by yourself.

Thomas: Was I in my home?

Boykin: Yes, you were at your house. You don't remember being at your house?

Thomas: I don't remember what's happened.

Boykin: Okay, do you remember coming home that night? That Saturday night? Or afternoon of whenever you got there?

Author's note: The next four or five questions and answers reveal quite clearly that Thomas just doesn't remember, and it appears very little information will come forward. Then, Cheryl says this:

Thomas: Uh, uh, my mind is so blank. I can't remember what's happened. I haven't tried to remember 'cause I don't want to be scared.

Clark: MMM.

Author's note: At this point, the investigators again probe for any memory Cheryl might have concerning Saturday night, mentioning her friend Nancy, and a fellow named Larry that Thomas had supposedly had a date with, but again, she's having trouble navigating through it. Then, the detectives mention a disco called Big Daddy's, and here is their exchange:

Boykin: Do you remember having a date, Cheryl, Saturday?

Thomas: MM

Boykin: Going out to Big Daddy's?

Thomas: Big Daddy's?

Clark: That's the disco lounge out here on the parkway, do you know where that is?

Thomas: Big Daddy's. Is that, is that um, is that uh, that two, two different places…

Clark: Dance floors.

Thomas: Uh huh.

Author's note: After additional questions were put to her, which did not produce any significant clues the investigators could use, Cheryl asked if they've caught the man who did this. Clark and Boykin said no, but that they were working on it, and that's why it was so important that they talk to her. Finishing out the Q&A, Cheryl asked the detectives several questions (sparked by a question from Detective Clark) which they happily responded to, knowing it would put her at ease.

Clark: Do you remember your cat?

Thomas: I remember I had a cat.

Clark: Uh huh.

Thomas: She's sorta fat 'cause she's gonna have babies.

Clark: Yeah, well, I gave the cat to Nancy. Nancy's taking care of him.

Thomas: Okay. Is my house all empty?

Clark: Uh, no, it's, uh, your house is fine.

Thomas: Is my ... who's staying at my house?

Clark: Uh, I don't think anybody is, right now.

Thomas: I hope it's safe.

Clark: It's safe, uh, we went back in and straightened everything back up for you and everything, everything's fine.

Thomas: Did anything happen at my house?

Clark: Well, that's where you got hurt.

Thomas: It is.

Author's note: After a few more additional exchanges, the detectives concluded the interview and told her to rest so that she could get better.

What follows is a brief exchange between Karen Chandler and the investigators. More lucid than her sorority sister and Cheryl Thomas, here's a portion of their exchange:

Boykin: Karen?

Chandler: MM.

Boykin: How're you doing? I'm Investigator Boykin with the police department and this is Investigator Clark with the sheriff's department. I talked with you briefly on Sunday, do you remember that?

Chandler: In the emergency room?

Boykin: Yes.

Chandler: When I was kind of throwing up and I was in there?

Boykin: Yes, uh huh. You remember that?

Chandler: (Indiscernible.)

Boykin: Uh, can you add any additional information to what you told us?

Chandler: I don't remember what I was saying at first, the only reason I think I thought it was a man was maybe that I heard a voice or something of a man.

Boykin: Now did we ask you uh.

Chandler: I thought it was a kind of a young man, I didn't think it was an old man.

Boykin: And you told us he was white.

Chandler: Um…

Boykin: Do you remember telling us?

Chandler: I don't know, I think so.

Boykin: Okay. Can you tell us … uh, what you remember about the incident, when you were in your room asleep?

Chandler: No sir, I remember, I mean I don't remember anything until, I remember the feeling of being on a stretcher and taking me outside to the ambulance, that's all I remember.

Boykin: You don't remember being struck?

Chandler: MMM.

Boykin: When you woke up, or what do you remember when you … were you knocked out, you think?

Chandler: The first thing that I remember is being in the ambulance in the roll away and remember hearing Kathy in the ambulance too. Then I remember being in the emergency room and kind of talking and throwing up.

Boykin: Okay. I understand you're going home Friday?

Chandler: Uh, I think so. (laughing)

Boykin: I tell you what, we won't bother you anymore today, but at a later date, when you're feeling better, we'll try to talk to you again. Uh, it's very important, uh, maybe you can remember something later on, and right now we don't want to bother you, let you get your rest, but uh, if you do remember anything, would you advise your mother or maybe a nurse here and maybe they'd contact us.

Chandler: Okay.

Boykin: Okay?

Chandler: Okay.

Boykin: Okay, hope you feel better here, thank you ma'am.

Author's note: What follows is a report from the Tallahassee Police Department and their interview of Carla Jean Black about her encounter with the spiraling downward Ted Bundy at Sherrod's, a disco next door to the Chi Omega sorority house that Bundy was known to frequent. The Black and Bundy interaction occurred only hours prior to the murders at Chi Omega. Carla Jean Black sat down with investigators on October 18, 1978.

NARRATIVE SUMMARY

October 18, 1978, 3:58 p.m. to 5:40 p.m., Tallahassee Police Department, C.I.D.

Interview with Carla Jean Black, 518 West Park Avenue.

The above witness is a F.S. U. student and a part-time employee for the F.S.U. Registrar, Graduation Department.

Ms. Black was in Sherrod's from 12:30 a.m. on January 15, 1978, until the business closed at approximately 2:00 a.m. that same date.

The purpose of this interview is to determine if Ms. Black has information pertaining to the homicides which occurred at 661 West Jefferson Street in the early a.m. of January 15, 1978. Also, to show Ms. Black a lineup containing known suspects to determine if she had seen any of the person(s) at Sherrod's on the date of the homicides.

According to Ms. Black, at about 12:30 a.m. on January 15, 1978, she and a sorority sister of hers, Valerie Stone, went to Sherrod's. They entered into the premises and, eventually, after getting a drink, she was standing around the area in the N.E. portion of the building, the area that has an exit directly adjacent to the Chi-O House.

Ms. Black's attention was drawn to a subject who appeared out of place, that is, he did not fit in with the typical college crowd. His dress and age, along with his appearance, i.e. greasy looking appearance, made him stand out to her.

Moreover, this subject kept staring at her, and she was afraid he would ask her to dance. Ms. Black was able to observe this subject from 15-30 minutes in a lighted area near the dance floor.

Ms. Black states that the subject kept staring at her and that she would look out the corner of her eye to see if he was still staring. When Ms. Black first noticed the subject making eye contact with her she states that it appeared flirtatious, but after a while she began to notice his actions more and that she became uncomfortable.

Ms. Black states that he kept staring at her, along with many other persons, and that his mannerisms seemed to be more a "rude type of looking" "that he appeared to be smirking" or "that he felt superior" or a "I know something that you don't know attitude." A combination of sexual overtones along with the overtone of aloofness.

When one girl walked by, he completely turned around and looking at the girl's posterior. Ms. Black is positive of where he was looking. Ms. Black describes this girl as attractive, possible blond, fair complexion, not fat nor skinny, about 5'4", 155 pounds wearing what appeared to be Levi type jeans and a sweater. Ms. Black states that she does not believe she would recognize the girl again, because she was observing the strange acting subject more than the girl.

Ms. Black observed the subject in three different areas during the time that she was in Sherrod's. First, when she entered into Sherrod's, she observed him near the front bar area directly front of the entrance from Jefferson Street, pretty dark area. Second, for the longest period in the N.E. section leaning against a wall near the dance floor. This is where she observed him staring at her and other people, lighted.

Thirdly, after he finally left the second area, to her relief, she later went to the ladies' room and he was standing east of the door to the ladies room, pretty dark.

Author's note: Black goes on to describe how Bundy was dressed and was able to identify him from a photograph shown to her. Indeed, she said, "To me that's him, looking at the picture brings back the same memories from that night, an eerie feeling."

Bundy, who would ultimately reject a life-sentence offer from the state of Florida (he would have had to stand up in court and admit to the murders), was convicted in two trials and put to death on January 24, 1989, for the murder of Kimberly Diane Leach. Of course, his death did not end the discussions of Bundy and his reign of terror. In fact, newspapers around the country scrambled to put their own mark on the closing of this dark saga, and no less so for the newspapers in the Northwest, as well as Utah, Colorado, and Florida. Because of the suffering Bundy caused in these states, it was especially fitting they do so.

Author's note: What follows are excerpts from an article published by the Tacoma News Tribune on February 20, 1989; only 27 days after Bundy was put to death. People had been sending letters of condolence to the grief-stricken Bundy family; family members that I consider were truly victims of Bundy's rampage as well. In it, Louise speaks of the process that took her son's life, as well as the horrible reality after Ted made his confessions.

"I can go along with people believing in the death penalty, but you can't be happy about it. It isn't to be a joyous celebration. When his confessions came out, it was all like a blow right between the eyes. This was not the Ted we had raised, we never saw anything to indicate it. We did everything parents of the 50s and 60s did."

Author's note: The article ends with a portion of a letter Ted penned to his parents the evening prior to his execution. In it, Bundy says:

"Nothing I can say can ease your pain. It is a terrible thing, I know, but I have to try to make it right, to tell the truth."

Author's note: What follows are excerpts from an editorial from the Tacoma News Tribune that was published on July 3, 1986, some 2 ½ years prior to Bundy's execution, and it, no doubt, accurately reflects most of their readers' feelings. Indeed, many folks, from Seattle to Tallahassee, just wanted Ted Bundy dead.

Bundy's Reprieve Delays Justice Convicted killer Ted Bundy, who left a trail of death from Washington to Florida, now has escaped an appointment with justice for the second time. He should not escape again, Bundy was given the benefit of fair trial. He was duly found guilty and sentenced to die for the horribly brutal murders of two college coeds and a 12-year-old girl. He remains arrogant and unrepentant, so manipulative and petulant that his jailors are remarkably unanimous in their desire to throw the switch.

"Justice delayed is justice denied" usually refers to a defendant's right to a fair trial. It also sums up perfectly, however, the effect of further delay in sending Ted Bundy to his fate.

An important question has been answered about the Slasher Movie, Black Christmas, and why Ted Bundy used the name

Chris Hagen when he arrived in Florida. In my opinion, the circumstantial evidence is quite strong, and it has forever settled it, at least in my own mind. What follows in the second paragraph below is what I wrote about the film in The Trail of Ted Bundy, and the latest discovery:

Just when you think you've discovered just about everything there is to know about a particular case, something else leaps up and surprises you. When that something which pops up has to do with a case as infamous as the Ted Bundy murders, it's always a very good thing. What follows is from my second book on the Ted Bundy case, *The Trail of Ted Bundy: Digging up the Untold Stories.*

"On December 20, 1974, *Black Christmas*, a Canadian "slasher" film, was released (for perhaps a somewhat limited release) in the United States. It was based on a series of murders that occurred in Montreal, and the movie depicts the killing, one by one, of a houseful of sorority sisters. Of course, it's unknown if Ted Bundy ever saw this film, and by Christmastime in 1974, he'd been murdering women for almost a year. It is known, however, that Bundy later told authorities it might behoove them to stake out theaters showing slasher films when they're looking for killers. Bundy, who knew quite a bit about avoiding detection, was no doubt onto something."

With that statement, the question of whether or not Ted Bundy saw a movie that was right up his murderous ally was put to rest, no reason to think about it further. Then, on December 16, 2016, an individual with the user name Maz U.K. contacted me on the blog I chair at Executed Today about Ted Bundy, and passed off the following information:

December 7, 2016 at 8:41 pm

"Hello Kevin, I just recently watched the 1975 *(Author's note: Maz meant 1974)* movie, Black Christmas, and discovered something that could be quite significant regarding Ted Bundy and his killings in Florida.

As you might know, the film is about a Sorority house, which is terrorized by a stranger who goes on to murder the sorority sisters *(Author's note: Reminiscent of Ted Bundy & Chi Omega?)*.

Not much of a coincidence, you might think, but what about this: the name Chris Hagen is mentioned in the movie. Wasn't that the exact name used as an alias by Ted Bundy, when living in Florida? It would seem to me that Bundy not only watched this film, but actually got the idea of a name he could use from it. What do you think?

See for yourself! Watch the movie from 19:45 minutes in."

Maz then gave a link to the YouTube site, and sure enough, at the aforementioned spot in the film, the name Chris Hagen pops up (at least, this is what my ears told me) as the boyfriend of one of the sorority sisters! Now, soon after this, I heard from an individual that the name is actually Chris Hayden, and after checking it out a bit further, I believe this is correct. That said, it is my absolute belief that not only did Ted Bundy see *Black Christmas*, but he also took the name Chris Hagen *purposely*, because it was in the film, *or he believed he heard it in the film.* Can any of this be proven? Of course, not. In my view, there just isn't any way that Ted Bundy pulled that name out of the air. No, he had to have seen the film.

THE TESTIMONY

Louise Cannon and Ted Bundy

Utah

Louise Cannon, of Salt Lake City, Utah, knew Ted Bundy through numerous interactions with him as a teller at the Bank of Salt Lake which sat on the corner of 2nd South and 1300 East (today it's the Key Bank). Near the University of Utah, it catered to an innumerable number of students and faculty, as it offered free checking to those at the university. Bundy began using this bank in 1974, and it was at this time when he first took notice of Louise Cannon. Being in her twenties, slim, with long dark hair that nearly reached her waist, she was just the type Bundy sought out to either kill or to date socially. In her case, it appears he wanted to get to know her with no intention of killing her, and the following stories seem to confirm that.

Anyway, it was Bundy that sought out the interaction with Louise and not the other way around. Indeed, because Bundy was ever observing people wherever he went, he most likely caught sight of her one day and decided to make it his business to get to know her. Indeed, Louise said, Bundy, who came into the bank two or three times a week, always got in her line "no matter how long the line was." It is important to note that when Bundy first started banking there in 1974, he was living at 565 First Avenue. After his October 1975 arrest for the kidnapping of Carol DaRonch, he moved to

364 Douglas Avenue, which is situated diagonally across the street from the bank, and as such, was in walking distance for Bundy, and she saw him often.

To Louise Cannon, Bundy looked like a regular guy. Her coworker, a bit older than Louise, perceived real problems with Ted. Whenever Bundy came into the bank, she actually put up a closed sign in her lane, and ducked down behind the counter. When Louise asked her about this, saying Bundy was just a nice college kid, she responded, "No, he's not nice! I can't stand to look at him. There's something wrong with his eyes; he's a killer!" She believed her superiors wouldn't like that she was avoiding Bundy, so she told Louise, "They can fire me if they want to, I won't wait on him." Once Bundy was exposed to the world as a killer, she remarked to Louise, "I told you so!"

On occasion, Louise came in to work at noon, and once the bank's lobby closed at 5:00 p.m., she worked the drive-through until 6:00 p.m. or later. This drive-through also had a walk-up lane which Bundy would sometimes use, and the two would talk during the transaction. One night, during the wintertime, Louise spotted Bundy cleaning the snow off her car, and, as she came out after locking up, Bundy asked her if she wanted to get a cup of coffee at a shop a few doors down. Louise agreed, and the two walked down the narrow alley to the coffee shop. Louise mentioned it was dark as they walked, but unlike with Georgann Hawkins, Bundy did not attack her. Afterward, they made their way back to the bank where Louise got into her car. Before they left, Bundy finished clearing the snow off her car, and Louise drove away. Bundy continued on to his apartment.

One day in 1975, Bundy called her at the bank and said, "Can you do me a favor? Go in and change my address to my attorney's address." When she questioned him why, Bundy responded "I'm in jail. I guess you haven't been watching the news." The next time Louise saw Bundy inside the bank, she said, no doubt in an upbeat manner, "You're a TV star." Bundy, in an obviously irritated tone, said, "Just cash the check".

Once it became known that Bundy was the individual the authorities were looking at as being responsible for the missing and murdered women of Utah, Louise was moved to the Sugar House branch, at the direction and assistance of a relative of hers who owned the bank. Bundy, after discovering she was no longer there, actually telephoned her at work and asked her about it. Louise was able to pass it off as just a normal procedure, and that she'd be working at all three branches and always on different days of the week. Indeed, she told him, she didn't know until the morning which branch she was going to be working that day. It was a lie, of course, but her safety was of the utmost concern, and she understood that would help to keep Bundy at bay.

One of the strangest, and perhaps most significant, things she told me about was an accidental run-in with Bundy which she had long before he was a suspect in the case. It was October 18, 1974, between 8:00 and 8:30 p.m., and Louise was meeting her friends at a bar known as Widow McCoy's, located at 3950 South Highland Avenue. Today, there's a newer Widow McCoy's right down the road. When Louise came through the door, Ted was sitting at the bar alone, sipping a drink. When he saw her, he said, "Hi Louise" and Louise said, "Hi" in return. On any other night, Ted would no doubt have chatted her up. After the quick greeting, Louise kept walking toward the table where her friends were waiting. A few minutes later, Bundy slid off the bar stool and left. What Louise didn't know, but would calculate later, was that she saw Bundy not only on the same night that Melissa Smith was abducted, but she saw him only two hours before the girl went missing. The distance between the original Widow McCoy's and the Pepperoni Pizza Place, where Melissa had been that night, was only a few blocks away and could be driven in a matter of minutes. A witness would later testify that Bundy had been there, sitting in a booth behind her, and that he left soon after Melissa walked out the door.

Louise also mentioned about the time Bundy had accidently left some of his law books and other school materials in the bank. The bank, which encountered such incidents from time to time, would always place such property on an open shelf within the bank so that customers would see it as they entered. However, Bundy never came back into the bank as long as Louise was there, and when she left for the other branch, the books remained on the shelf.

Officer Chip Springer

Florida

In February of 1978, at the time of the Chi Omega attacks, Chip Springer was working as an operating room tech at Tallahassee Memorial Hospital, and was present in the OR when the victims of Ted Bundy were treated. Jaws were wired back together, cheekbones were worked on, and the brains of the injured were monitored for swelling and bleeding. Doctors from their respective specialties worked well together, collectively providing the best possible care for the victims.

Even though Springer was working as an OR Tech, he

had applied to become a police officer with Florida State University campus police, but the process was slow and he had to be patient. The day after the murders of Margaret Bowman and Lisa Levy at Chi Omega, however, an emergency hiring order was issued and he was told to report the next day. Before he reported for duty, they asked if he owned a firearm, and he replied that he did. After conferring with them, he was allowed to use it as his service weapon.

During our phone conversation of July 14, 2016, he stressed how much Tallahassee was in turmoil because of the murders, and having written about the city's state of mind after the killings in my first book, I quickly agreed. The fact that someone would enter a quiet sorority house in the middle of the night, attack four innocent college women, killing two of them, created a nightmarish experience in the minds of many. It also had an effect on the remaining FSU students who were still housed on campus, especially the female population. Chip Springer would learn this first-hand in the coming days.

Responding to a nighttime medical emergency call from Reynolds Hall on the FSU campus, some two weeks after the murders at Chi Omega, Springer entered the second-floor hall and hollered out "man on the floor." Knocking on one door, Springer said the door opened just a couple of inches, and immediately the barrel of a .357 magnum Colt Python revolver was pointing in his direction, followed by the voice of a female asking, "Who is it?" Springer identified himself as an FSU police officer which calmed the frightened young woman. Chip Springer believed that many students remaining on campus obtained handguns for protection, most likely from distraught parents.

He also mentioned that because of the lack of air conditioning, many of the women wore next to nothing in the evening and had a habit of studying in the hall. This was often what the officers ran into if they had to make a run to the women's dorm. In fact, Springer once was confronted with a completely nude woman, who quickly returned to her room as soon as she saw him. This practice of studying in the halls did not resume until months after Bundy's capture.

Around mid-morning on February 13, 1978, Officers Chip Springer and Mike Kelly were dispatched to 806 West Georgia Street to check out a FSU van parked in the driveway of Beatrice Hampton's residence. It was very quickly confirmed that it was the university's media center van, which had been reported stolen a few days earlier. Peering into the rear window, Springer observed a lot of dirt and leaves inside. Within moments, the officers radioed back requesting that Steve Hooker, the captain of the investigations division, be sent to the scene. Along with Hooker, others made their way to the van and soon it was impounded and towed to another location. Further investigation revealed that Bundy left no fingerprints in the van, but in addition to the dirt and leaves, blood was also located.

Several months later, a pest control worker, spraying the outside of the house directly across the street from the rear portion of Chi Omega, found a stack of women's purses discarded in the backyard of the home, and contacted the university police. It was discovered that most, if not all, of these purses had been stolen from Sherrod's, the disco next door to Chi Omega which Bundy frequented. Without question, I believe this was the work of the killer.

Lastly, Springer said that when he had to return to the room which Bundy had occupied at The Oak at 409 College Avenue, the place had been swept clean (like the van, no finger prints had been found there by the forensic team), and everything except the television was missing. On the back of the TV, Springer found a knife which had been taped to it. Was this Bundy? We will never know.

Sandra Schwartz, who may have been a target of Ted Bundy in Pocatello, Idaho, around the same time that Bundy was known to have abducted and murdered Lynette Culver in May 1975. Courtesy of Sandra Schwartz

Sandra Schwartz

Idaho

Whenever one thinks of the murders Bundy committed, two things come to mind: 1. How many women or young girls did Bundy actually kill?, and 2. How many others did he unsuccessfully attempt to abduct? Bundy, even when naming his victims and freely admitting to their murders, still refused to talk about all of them. We also know that there were women that Bundy failed to abduct, just because it didn't work out for various reasons, as in his hunt in Pocatello, Idaho, until he succeeded in snatching young Lynette Culver. As to these exact numbers, these are two questions which will remain with us forever.

That said, over the years, I've heard from many women (and even some men) who maintain that they had encountered Bundy during his years of actively committing murder. Within official records, I've been able to determine where Bundy was at certain times, and from that information, have been able to make a pretty good determination if it was even possible for the killer to have crossed their paths. Other times, I'm not so lucky, as there isn't any way to check out the facts. In one case, a woman contacted me about a VW pulling over to the side of the road in Seattle in 1975, saying the driver had tried to coax her into his car. Because she had stated this on a blog I chair, most folks answered her saying it would be impossible for Bundy to have been there at that time, but I referred to my book, *The Bundy Murders,* to check it out. Lo and behold, I found a brief mention that Bundy was back home in Seattle, only for a week or so, during the exact same time frame that this woman was proclaiming he tried to abduct her. While this doesn't prove anything, it does raise the credibility factor to the degree that one can honestly consider it. So it is, with the following story.

What follows are the words of Sandra Schwartz, who private messaged me on Facebook. After we had talked for a while, I knew I wanted to add her testimony to this third book of this trilogy of books I've written about the Bundy murders. We can't say for certainty that the man that did this was Ted Bundy, but we can't completely rule him out either, for two reasons. First of all, she's adamant that this man was Bundy, she both saw him and heard his voice, and her mention of the voice is of particular interest to me. This occurred in the same area where, shortly thereafter, Bundy snatched Lynette Culver. Indeed, we know from the record that Bundy was a creature of habit, from filling up at the same gas stations in the same cities while trolling for victims, to sometimes hunting victims in the same areas. It is entirely possible that his May 6, 1974, visit to Pocatello may not have been his only one. What follows is Sandra's story in her own words.

"My name is Sandra Schwartz. In 1974, I went by the name of Sandy Copelin (my maiden name). One afternoon, in late Summer or Fall of 1974, I was walking home from Westwood Village Mall, near my home. A car pulled up alongside me; it was a darker colored sedan-maybe maroon or brownish (not a Volkswagen). The passenger window was already down. The driver leaned over to ask if I would take part in a survey. My father had taught me to be very suspicious of strangers, so I took note of his face and voice. His questions seemed silly. I then glanced down and his tape recorder was not running. I told him he was weird and walked away. I was ready to run if he got out of his car, but, thankfully, he sped away. When I reached home, I relayed the story to my mother; she was glad I got home safely. It wouldn't be until much later when Ted Bundy became infamous that I would recognize him. And it was only a few months later (*Author's note: after Sandra's incident*) that he took Lynette Culver from Alameda Jr. High, just a few blocks from my home. He killed her at the Holiday Inn on Bench Road (it's now the Clarion) not far from my high school."

That she studied this man's face *and* voice is, in my opinion, a good sign that this might very well have been Ted Bundy. That she was answering his questions and then saw the recorder wasn't running, means something was up with this guy, and she knew it. None of this proves it was Ted Bundy, but in my view, you can't rule it out either; and especially so because of her statement of face and voice. The only information that could scuttle it in the minds of some is that the man was driving something other than a VW, which could be problematic for some, as his car at the time was a VW. However, while that's true, it may also be true that for whatever reason, he borrowed the car of a friend to take what could have been a quick day trip only. In any event, whomever this was that stopped Sandra did so for reasons other than conducting an interview; in an area where we know Bundy would be hunting (possibly again?) in the near future. We will never know for certain if this was Ted Bundy, but because of his penchant for being an active mobile killer, I certainly can't rule it out. It is for this reason that I've added Sandra's story to the book.

Greg Rose and Lynda Ann Healy

Oregon

In 1974, Greg Rose was a disc jockey at KJIB 99.5 FM in Portland, Oregon. Each morning, and twice more throughout the day, KJIB would receive live on-air updates from Northwest Ski Promotions in Seattle, detailing conditions in commercial ski areas in their neck of the woods, including Mt. Hood, Mt. Bachelor, Mt. Baker, and Snoqualmie Pass for the station's listeners venturing in search for the perfect slope. As the midday deejay, Rose answered the late morning call from Northwest Ski Promotions, which is how he became acquainted with Lynda Ann Healy, one of Northwest's correspondents and a senior at the University of Washington, who spent her weekday mornings reciting the ski reports from across the region. Through this crossing of paths, via telephone, Greg Rose and Lynda Ann Healy got to know each other. Although they never met in person, as Greg related to me in an email, he "spoke to her frequently on the phone, and we sometimes exchanged 'snappy patter' between ourselves prior to the report." It was clear from his email, and our phone conversation later that week, that he and Lynda shared a cordial and professional rapport. Rose regrets that he never had the opportunity to travel to Seattle, for they had talked about meeting for a cup of coffee; a meeting that would have allowed them to put a face to the voice each had come to know over the phone.

On Thursday morning, January 31, 1974, Greg and Lynda were having their usual conversation prior to the live report she delivered on KJIB. The weekend was fast approaching, and Greg, making conversation, asked her what she was planning to do over the weekend. She had "stuff" to do, she told him, errands to run, and of course, the constant studying. It was all so very normal. When they said goodbye for the day, neither he nor Lynda had any idea what was about to transpire, especially that this would be their last conversation.

When word reached KJIB that Lynda Healy was missing, Greg Rose feared something was wrong. She wasn't the type of person, he believed, that would just take off and leave people hanging; she was too professional and too considerate. Those who really knew Lynda Healy, and interacted with her on a daily basis, echoed the same firm opinion of her, that this was not something that Lynda would do. For all of their positive thinking, and hoping that Lynda would return home, it wouldn't take long before they all believed foul play was involved in her disappearance. During our phone conversation of August 5, 2016, Greg Rose told me that the concern that something terrible had happened to Lynda came to him fairly quickly. He couldn't imagine she would have vanished on her own, and he couldn't help but make the connection between her odd disappearance and a book he'd both read and enjoyed in his earlier years. It was about a hopelessly awkward young man who collects butterflies and then, ultimately, he determines to "collect" a beautiful woman whom he could never possibly hope to attract in his real life. It was, without question, a dark novel, and was appropriately entitled, *The Collector*, by John Fowles, a work which Time magazine pronounced "A superb novel … evil has seldom been so sinister." It became an instant hit around the globe, and as often happens with bestsellers, it was also made into a movie.

It would be some time before Greg Rose would learn what really happened to Lynda Ann Healy, and that it was Ted Bundy who killed her.

Bryan Severson purchased Ted Bundy's VW in 1975, but his dealings with him would stretch into the future as he was caught up in the investigation of the killer

Bryan Severson and Ted Bundy

Utah

In 1975, seventeen-year-old Bryan Severson was looking seriously for a car. Spotting an ad selling a 1968 VW Bug in the local newspaper, he made arrangements to visit the owner who lived in a rooming house at 565 First Avenue, near the University of Utah, in Salt Lake City. As he and a female friend climbed the stairs to the second floor, they had no idea who they were meeting or the significance of this transaction, nor what it would mean for Severson in the coming weeks and months.

As they reached the top of the steps, they turned to the right and knocked on the door marked number two. A moment later, a smiling Ted Bundy opened the door and invited them inside. In a telephone conversation I had with Severson on August 19, 2016, he told me Ted Bundy was nice and acted perfectly normal throughout their meeting. He also mentioned how exceedingly clean Bundy kept his apartment; an observation which had also been noted in a police report by Detective Jerry Thompson. While there, Severson's friend asked Bundy if she could use the restroom. Ted agreed, and then led her through his bedroom to the bathroom. If Severson had not yet, as they left the apartment that day, made up his mind to purchase Bundy's car, he soon would.

On September 19, 1975, Ted Bundy climbed into his VW for the last time and traveled south to Sandy, Utah, to finalize the deal with Severson, who couldn't wait to have his new car. When Ted arrived, he discovered that Severson needed to wait a couple of hours for his mother to return home so that he could cash the $800 check he'd received from his loan company. Extending a gesture of hospitality, he suggested they go inside his home and wait. Naturally, it wasn't ideal to wait on the front steps for two hours. However, Severson recalls that after only five or ten minutes, Bundy became noticeably uncomfortable, so they went back outside to the front steps. This was not the only odd reaction Severson would see about Bundy. When his police officer neighbor came out of his house, Severson went over to speak with him, and Bundy began showing signs of nervousness. Although noticeable, Severson stated that he didn't give it a lot of thought at the time. Later, of course, it would all make perfect sense.

Bundy also did something that had nothing to do with nervousness, but which did strike Severson as a bit strange. A female neighbor, who was also a friend of Severson, came walking down the sidewalk and Bundy locked his eyes on her and kept up that gaze the entire time she moved all the way down the block.

Once the deal was done, Bundy thanked him for buying his car. Because Bundy had shown up without anyone to drive him home, Severson gave him a lift back to his apartment. Bundy also told Severson that he should just drive the VW but not transfer the title as the tags wouldn't expire until January of 1976, a move that would allow Severson to delay licensing and tax payments. Given the understanding that Bundy never made suggestions to benefit other people when his own intentions were at stake, the real reason for his offer undoubtedly had more to do with making it more difficult for the cops to locate and bring the car in to search it for additional evidence. Severson, not wanting to drive around a vehicle that didn't officially belong to him, registered it within the next few days. Severson also told me, that on the night he bought the car, he took it out for a drive, and was almost immediately pulled over by a patrolman for exceeding the 25-mph speed limit. The officer, not wanting to stick the kid with a ticket, let him off with a warning, and never asked to see his registration. None of this would matter, because, as it would turn out, the car was only going to be his for a very short time.

Several weeks after Severson received the title to his car, police from the Salt Lake County Sheriff's Office showed up in force with three or four patrol cars and a tow truck. They needed his car back, they told the surprised high school kid, and they promised him they'd have it back to him in two weeks at the latest. Not wanting to stand in the way of the police, he turned over the keys, but despite the request that he turn over the title, he refused to do so. Indeed, Severson told this writer that he was so insistent they not get it that he hid the document in the cuff of one of his pants that were hanging up in his closet.

Two weeks came and went and there was still no car. When Severson contacted them, he was informed that the car was not legally his. It was discovered that Bundy had given the title to Beehive Bail Bonds for quick cash after his arrest for the Carol DaRonch abduction. Apparently, the title he had given to Severson was a copy. It was also clear that the police had openly lied to him; that they never had any intentions of returning his car. Not knowing what else to do, Severson got his dad involved and the two of them went to see an attorney. It took six months of wrangling with the authorities before he finally received a call from his lawyer that a check for $800 was waiting for him to be picked up. Once Bryan had the money in his hands, he immediately went to the loan office and paid off a car that he never really owned.

Knowing what kind of experience, he'd had with the sheriff's department, I asked him if he'd ever interacted with Utah Detective Jerry Thompson, who was lead investigator in the

Bundy case, and if so, what was his experience with him? He said Jerry was very nice (no surprise here), and that he had dealt with him fairly. Not only did Bryan Severson talk with Utah lead investigator Thompson, but he also had some dealings with Colorado Investigator, Michael Fisher, who he also found to be a nice guy, as well.

But Severson's journey didn't end here. After Bundy was transferred to Colorado to stand trial for the murder of Caryn Campbell (he had abducted her from the Wildwood Inn in Snowmass, Colorado), Mike Fisher came to Severson and presented him with a subpoena to appear in the Aspen, Colorado courthouse and testify against Bundy. Although he was agreeable to the idea, he didn't want it to cost him any money, and Fisher assured him he'd take care of everything.

When the time came to leave, Severson flew to Denver, and then took a shuttle flight in a smaller plane to Aspen. On the evening he arrived, along with kidnapping victim Carol DaRonch, he went to a dinner of steak and lobster with Mike Fisher and Jerry Thompson. After the meal was consumed, they went to a nearby hotel and gathered together in a conference room with other detectives, and members of the media, including newspaperman, Richard Larsen, who would eventually go on to write his bestseller, *Bundy: The Deliberate Stranger*.

Severson told me that he sat beside Carol DaRonch as the group was seated around a long table. In the midst of small talk, she mentioned how glad she was to have gotten away from Bundy. At some point, Richard Larsen came over and sat down beside Severson, introducing himself, telling young Severson that he was writing a book about the case. It was obvious he wanted to hear everything Bryan could tell him. Always willing to be helpful, Severson had but one request:

"Don't use my real name." Later, after the book had been published, however, a friend contacted him and told him that he's in Larsen's book. Understandably upset, Bryan found out that Larsen had only changed several letters of his last name, hardly disguising his true identity.

When it came time to give his testimony in the old Aspen courthouse, Bryan once again came face-to-face with Ted Bundy. In fact, Bundy, being involved in his own defense, cross-examined Severson about the photographs the police had taken of the car he sold to Bryan, stating they were not the same vehicle at all, seemingly suggesting the Utah authorities were attempting to pull a fast one on Bundy. Severson, however, quickly pointed out where a girl he knew had taken some fingernail paint and painted the windshield washer nozzles fluorescent pink. Although an odd thing to do, it became indisputable evidence that the car Bundy sold to Bryan Severson was in fact the same vehicle.

After Bundy's second and final escape from the lax Colorado jailers, Mike Fisher asked Severson if he needed protection just in case Bundy came back to Salt Lake City, but he told Fisher he did not. However, Bryan mentioned to me that for a while, at least, he never answered the front door without having a knife in his hands, presumably hidden from view.

Lastly, it is of interest to note that Bryan attended the same school with Melissa Smith at Hillcrest High School. He remembers her as a sweet girl.

AFTERWORD

With the completion of this third book, my in-depth and long-lasting mental, emotional, and physical journey into the Ted Bundy saga now comes to an end. Having written some six hundred plus pages in this trilogy, where, in my view, every aspect of the subject has been covered with first, *The Bundy Murders*, an in-depth biography of the killer, and then, *The Trail of Ted Bundy*, a revisiting of the sites and locations pertaining to the case, as well as much new testimony, and now with the release of *The Bundy Secrets: Hidden Files on America's Worst Serial Killer*, all that I have wanted to say has now been said; at least, it is the last I'll be saying about the Bundy case in book format.

Depending on future discoveries, or perhaps some other new or strange revelation, what has already been discovered by previous Bundy biographers will never be surpassed. Indeed, when writing my first book on the case, I uncovered some long-hidden secrets about a number of the murders that proved to be significant. Not only was I surprised by this, but greatly pleased, as more than a few folks I knew were trying to talk me out of writing about Bundy, but I persevered anyway. I'm glad that I did, for without the publication of the first book, the two additional books wouldn't exist either.

I am aware that the case of the Ted Bundy murders is etched within my being in such a way that I know it will be permanent for as long as I live. That's the key thing, isn't it? As long as I live. As such, as a historian (not a term one might think of applying to a writer of mostly true crime), I'm happy to know that this trilogy into the world that was Ted Bundy will be available to readers and researchers for many, many years to come. Knowing this does put a smile on my face.

I want to thank all of you who have journeyed with me through the years. I've enjoyed all of the feedback you've given me, whether it's on Facebook, the blog I chair at Executed Today, or at any other site or venue we happen to meet. We all share a common bond because of our interest in this most unusual, interesting, and very sad case, and I always welcome your contact. Indeed, I'm happy to call all of you friends.

Thanks again!

Kevin

ACKNOWLEDGEMENTS

Even though this is a book primarily about the official record of the Bundy case, I still have numerous folks I'd like to mention, and thank, for helping me along the way.

I would like to thank the following people: Carol Bartholomew, who not only was of great assistance to me during the writing of my previous Bundy book, but she gave me the name of Louise Cannon; Louise Cannon, who so willingly shared her experience with Ted Bundy while she was a clerk in the bank Bundy used near the University of Utah; Bryan Severson, the young man mentioned in the official record that purchased Ted Bundy's VW in 1975. Not only did Bryan share his story with me, but he gave me an upfront look at his dealings with the investigators, and what it was like testifying at Bundy's trial in Colorado; Greg Rose, who allowed me to interview him concerning his connection with Lynda Ann Healy, and I very much appreciate his truthfulness and willingness to share the information; My friend and fellow writer, Fred Rosen, who passed my contact info along to Greg Rose, which made the interview possible; Chip Springer, who not only graciously allowed me to interview him so that I could tell his most interesting story, but he also corrected certain "facts" that I had inadvertently inserted into his story that were not exactly correct, and by doing so, he kept me on track; Sandra Schwartz, for the story of her possible encounter with Ted Bundy in the city of Pocatello, Idaho. Of all the individuals who have contacted me over the years with their own

"Bundy story," only several appeared credible to me, and Sandra's story is one of them; Robert J. Cook, who contacted me after having read my first two books about the case. Bob was a staff minister at Parkview Baptist Church (Kimberly Leach's church) from 1976-1980, and he told me that "Her funeral was one of the two most attended funerals during my time at Parkview. The other one was for a law enforcement officer who was murdered;" and lastly, I want to thank, for the last time in print, the investigators I've had the pleasure of working with over the years: Jerry Thompson of Utah, Mike Fisher of Colorado, Bob Keppel of Washington State, Don Patchen of Florida, Russ Reneau of Idaho, and retired FBI Special Agent Bill Hagmaier. Your help was invaluable.

If there are others out there that I've failed to thank (always a concern for the writer), I offer my heartfelt apology for the mistake, along with a big thank you for all your help.

ABOUT THE AUTHOR

Kevin M. Sullivan is the author of twelve books, a former contributing writer for *Snitch*, a now defunct weekly print newspaper devoted to issues of crime and the law, and a former contributor to the online site, *In Cold Blog*.

His books include: *The Bundy Murders: A Comprehensive History; The Trail of Ted Bundy: Digging Up the Untold Stories; Vampire: The Richard Chase Murders; Kentucky Bloodbath: Ten Bizarre Tales of Murder from the Bluegrass State; Custer's Road to Disaster: The Path to Little Bighorn; Shattering the Myth: Signposts on Custer's Road to Disaster;* and *Unnatural Causes*, co-authored with Gregg Olsen.

Use this link to sign up for advance notice
of new books from Kevin Sullivan
http://wildbluepress.com/AdvanceNotice

Word-of-mouth is critical to an author's long-term success.
If you appreciated this book please leave a review on the
Amazon sales page:
http://wbp.bz/bundysecretsa

Other WildBlue Press Books
By Kevin Sullivan

VAMPIRE: *The Richard Chase Murders*
http://wbp.bz/vampirea

KENTUCKY BLOODBATH: *Ten Bizarre Tales
of Murder From The Bluegrass State*
http://wbp.bz/kba

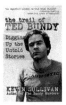

THE TRAIL OF TED BUNDY:
Digging Up The Untold Stories
http://wbp.bz/trailbundya

AVAILABLE NOW FROM WILDBLUE PRESS

Betrayal In Blue
by Burl Barer, Frank C. Girardot Jr, Ken Eurell

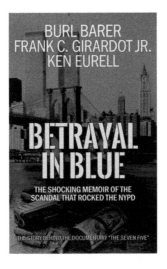

Adapted from Ken Eurell's shocking personal memoir, plus hundreds of hours of exclusive interviews with the major players, including former international drug lord, Adam Diaz, and Dori Eurell, revealing the truth behind what you won't see in the hit documentary THE SEVEN FIVE. Edgar Award winner Burl Barer once again teams with award-winning journalist Frank C. Girardot, Jr, and Eurell to bring you an astonishing story of greed and betrayal.

BETRAYAL IN BLUE
http://wbp.bz/bib
www.WildBluePress.com

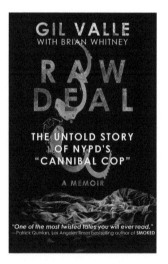

More True Crime You'll Love From WildBlue Press

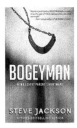

BOGEYMAN: He Was Every Parent's Nightmare by Steve Jackson *"A master class in true crime reporting. He writes with both muscle and heart."* (Gregg Olsen, New York Time bestselling author). A national true crime bestseller about the efforts of tenacious Texas lawmen to solve the cold case murders of three little girls and hold their killer accountable for his horrific crimes by New York Times bestselling author Steve Jackson. *"Absorbing and haunting!"* (Ron Franscell, national bestselling author and journalist)

wbp.bz/bogeyman

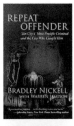

REPEAT OFFENDER by Bradley Nickell *"Best True Crime Book of 2015"* (Suspense Magazine) A "Sin City" cop recounts his efforts to catch one of the most prolific criminals to ever walk the neon-lit streets of Las Vegas. *"If you like mayhem, madness, and suspense, Repeat Offender is the book to read."* (Aphrodite Jones, New York Times bestselling author)

wbp.bz/ro

DADDY'S LITTLE SECRET by Denise Wallace *"An engrossing true story."* (John Ferak, bestselling author of Failure Of Justice, Body Of Proof, and Dixie's Last Stand) Daddy's Little Secret is the poignant true crime story about a daughter who, upon her father's murder, learns of his secret double-life. She had looked the other way about other hidden facets of his life - deadly secrets that could help his killer escape the death penalty, should she come forward.

wbp.bz/dls

BODY OF PROOF by John Ferak *"A superbly crafted tale of murder and mystery."* – (Jim Hollock, author of award-winning BORN TO LOSE) When Jessica O'Grady, a tall, starry-eyed Omaha co-ed, disappeared in May 2006, leaving behind only a blood-stained mattress, her "Mr. Right," Christopher Edwards, became the suspect. Forensic evidence gathered by CSI stalwart Dave Kofoed, a man driven to solve high-profile murders, was used to convict Edwards. But was the evidence tainted? A true crime thriller written by bestselling author and award-winning journalist John Ferak.

wbp.bz/bop